Olio

OLIO

Tyehimba Jess

WAVE BOOKS SEATTLE & NEW YORK

Published by Wave Books

www.wavepoetry.com

Copyright © 2016 by Tyehimba Jess

Illustrations by Jessica Lynne Brown

Wave Books titles are distributed to the trade by

Consortium Book Sales and Distribution

Phone: 800-283-3572 / SAN 631-760X

Library of Congress Cataloging-in-Publication Data

Jess, Tyehimba.

[Poems. Selections]

Olio / Tyehimba Jess. — First edition.

pages ; cm

ISBN 978-1-940696-22-5 (hardcover) —

ISBN 978-1-940696-20-1 (softcover)

I. Title.

PS3610.E874A6 2016

811'.6—dc23

2015026171

Crash at Crush image courtesy of The Texas Collection,

Baylor University. Photograph of Paul Laurence Dunbar

appears courtesy of the Ohio History Connection.

Photographs of Bert Williams and George Walker provided

by John Hay Library, Brown University Library.

Designed and composed by Quemadura

Printed in Canada

9 8 7 6 5 4 3 2 1

First Edition

Wave Books 053

olio \\'ō-lē-,ō\\

a : a miscellaneous mixture of heterogeneous elements; hodgepodge

b : a miscellaneous collection (as of literary or musical selections)

also: the second part of a minstrel show which featured a variety of performance acts and later evolved into vaudeville.

CONTENTS

* * * * * * * *

* * * * * * * *

* * * * * * * *

* * * * * * * *

Olio

INTRODUCTION

or

CAST

or

Owners of This Olio

* * * * * * * * *

JOHN WILLIAM "BLIND" BOONE (1864–1927)

Sprung from a Yankee bugler and a newly freed mother, his sight was sacrificed to encephalitis at the age of six months. Possessed by a prodigious memory, perfect pitch, and a particular partiality to piano, from which he sees and he sees and he sees . . .

HENRY "BOX" BROWN (1816–?)

One day, he got *carried away*—crate-wise. Slipped from slavery by mailing himself free to Philly. Motivated abolitionists and mesmerized the British for 25 years . . . returned to amaze America in 1875. Here, he blues the blackface in John Berryman's *Dream Songs*.

PAUL LAURENCE DUNBAR (1872–1906)

He of the *Lyrics of Lowly Life*. Maestro of *Majors and Minors*. Dayton's former elevator operator power-lifting literature. Liberator of verse through the golden cage/broiled rage of dialect. Singer of form when "We Wear the Mask" and signal of defiance "When Malindy Sings."

THE FISK JUBILEE SINGERS (1871–)

Our ensemble smuggles a cappella out of coffles. Fisk's first alumni choir sings circles through history's halo of fire.

ERNEST HOGAN (1865–1909)

Hogan holds claim to creating the Coon Song genre with "All Coons Look Alike to Me"—the million-selling hit of 1896. Early ragtime royalty—the first Black to produce and mount his own play on the Great White Way.

SISSIERETTA JONES (1868–1933)

They dubbed her "Black Patti." We thrall her Miss Jones. Hailing from Providence, the first Black Diva to croon in Carnegie. Led a worldwide tour of her eponymous Troubadours from 1896–1916.

SCOTT JOPLIN (1867–1917)

Ruler of Ragtime. Professor of Piano Prestidigitation. Saint of Syncopation. Ace of Ivory 88s.

MILLIE AND CHRISTINE MCKOY (1851–1912)

The Creator consigned the McKoys with the grace and grit to be conjoined twins. To be born into slavery. To be regularly inspected by physicians to verify their combined condition; to be leased to traveling freak tours at the age of two. When kidnapped to England at the age of three, their owner took their mother there as receipt to retrieve them back—and away from British liberty. Upon emancipation, they famously traveled the world until they bought their old plantation.

BOOKER T. WASHINGTON (1856–1915)

Booker Taliaferro; Taproot of Tuskegee Institute. Race Ambassador who trained up teachers in troops. He who drew up a compromised bucket of truce down in Atlanta to alleviate lynch mobs' rule. He who is nobody's fool. He who dances language note for note on the industrial soapbox. He who, even still, feels a twist in his dome for his folk who still till fields of poems.

"BLIND" TOM WIGGINS (1849–1908)

Tom was born autistic slave savant, possessing formidable piano skills. Under the lifelong "management" of his masters, the Bethunes, Wiggins played $1 million worth of tunes. He's family inheritance, bound from father to son to wife, until his Final Freedom on the other side . . .

BERT WILLIAMS (1874–1922) AND GEORGE WALKER (1872–1911)

Williams & Walker: theater pioneers. Self-produced stars of *Sons of Ham* and our dear homeys from their play *In Dahomey*. A diamond-studded comedic duo delivering duets of blackface delirium; a hog-tied hilarity freed from the rope. They conjure trope into cravat and cigar; they grind ash into laughter to smear over scars.

WILDFIRE, OR EDMONIA LEWIS (1844–1907)

Her mother Ojibwe, her father Maroon. Her chisel a language, each stone a new moon-bright canvas of Grecian marble waiting to spell out whose tale dwells inside its tomb—and how she'll strike them into our sight. Expatriate artist at age 20—escaped Yankee art markets to be free in Greece selling statuary for up to 50 Gs.

Fix your eyes on the flex of these first-generation-freed voices:
They coalesce in counterpoint, name nemeses, summon tongue to wit-ness.
Weave your own chosen way between these voices . . .

FISK JUBILEE PROCLAMATION

(CHORAL)

O sing unto the Lord a new song . . . (Psalm 96)

O, sing . . . undo the world with blued song

born from newly freed throats. Sprung loose from lungs

once bound within bonded skin. Scored from dawn

to dusk with coffle and lash. Every tongue

unfurled as the body's flag. Every breath

conjured despite loss we've had. Bear witness

to the birthing of our hymn from storied depths

of America's sin. Soul-worn psalms, blessed

in our blood through dark lessons of the past

struggling to be heard. Behold—the bold sound

we've found in ourselves that was hidden, cast

out of the garden of freedom. It's loud

and unbeaten, then soft as a newborn's face—

each note bursting loose from human bondage.

Dr. W. E. B. Du Bois, Editor

NAACP Crisis Magazine

70 Fifth Avenue

New York City, New York

April 1, 1927

Dear Dr. Du Bois,

Please accept these interviews, recorded to the best of my meager abilities, that portray the memories and last days of one Scott Joplin, piano player. Enclosed are testimonies to the pauper king of piano, who gave his last concert to his fellow infirmed just before his death on April Fools' Day, 1917, in the Manhattan State Hospital.

My own encounters with Mr. Joplin have been almost entirely secondhand. My personal contact with him was brief and unremarkable. Nevertheless, I submit my own story here as testimony to the origins and purpose of this research—and to the relevance of its musical subject.

My mother played Joplin's rags after each sunset on our small farm. She lived long enough for me to be able to recall the way her hands ruled the keyboard as if possessed when she traced his tunes beneath her fingertips; her eyes lost focus, then shut tight when she paid homage to his compositions upon our battered upright. I believe now that these tunes were a small escape for her, a refuge from the stifling circumstances of our southern Ohio town.

My father, a scraped-up scruff of a man, would fold in the hard edges of his face and come close as he could to a smile whenever she played his work. He'd known the composer back in Texarkana. While laying track and driving spikes on the rails, he'd met a fellow gandy dancer with unusual talents. When he sang the rhythm for the work crew, he'd always "trick up the rhythm" so the hammers would fall just a bit faster and surer on the rails. When the workday was done, this fellow would always seek out a piano to bring those rhythms to life with more color and depth. This piano player swore that his days of manual labor would be brief, and that he'd be traveling with his music soon. It turned out that his name was Scott. Later, when my father first met my mother as she played his music, he would swear he heard the ringing in the rails from his youth.

Our mother told us on more than one occasion that here was *our* voice unlocked from the keys. *Our* voice hammered on the strings. She did indeed sweat to make those tunes her own as much as Joplin's.

When pneumonia took her from us by my tenth birthday, I was only to be consoled by continually working his tunes like talismans on our piano as best I could with the instruction she'd given me and my siblings in the years before her death. Our piano slowly grew more ramshackle and detuned due to our increasingly austere conditions. My father, run weary by the loss of my mother and besieged by the need to support us, eventually sold off our piano—and bit by bit, all our remaining land. Ultimately he found it necessary to once again work the rails as he did as a younger man. However, swinging nine pound hammers proved too much for his heart, and soon we were left to fend for ourselves.

At a young age I was fortunate enough to earn admission to Lincoln University. After graduation, although still aspiring toward a more professional career, I eventually regarded my chances for employment to be more successful on the Pullman line. It was through this line of work that I was able to first visit New York City. I was walking on 22nd Street near Tin Pan Alley in December of 1916, when the sound of one of my mother's favorites, "The Strenuous Life," stopped me in my tracks. The player had the same phrasing, the same sense of *grave* and injection of *glissando* that my mother had drawn from deep within our piano's interior with each dusk. Investigating the source, I entered the Rosamond Lounge where in the fall of a yellow spotlight, seated at a dusty upright, was a small, shabby figure slowly nodding with the rhythm of his left hand. He concluded the tune and paused. While there was no applause, he nevertheless tipped his battered porkpie in the sparse crowd's direction.

He launched into the next tune—I could hear him rasp the title—"Bethena." This I had also heard my mother play—but while listening to the tune from what I had determined by that time to be the composer himself, I suddenly knew it in a way I hadn't ever imagined. Slower. Wrought. A window of broken windows, a celebration of sunlight held within. A writhing, and then a rapture. I remember hearing the last notes, some scattered applause. I remember this—that my eyes were closed, that I could almost see my mother in that darkness toiling, weeping over our ramshackle keyboard at home. That when I opened them again, the figure had retired from view, leaving nothing more than the abandoned piano onstage.

I waited for the maestro to reappear—I then went backstage to finally meet the maker of my mother's music. But to my alarm he had left the building altogether—and if I did not return to my Chicago-bound train immediately, I was going to miss it and be henceforth unemployed. The choice was tragic but necessary, and I vowed to track him down at the same address during my next sojourn to Manhattan.

And I did search for him vehemently upon my next berth in New York. He was nowhere to be found. I tried again and again, but still he eluded me. And then, in the early weeks of April, I read a small, perfunctory article in the *New York Times*. This was his final grace note; his life's work reduced to one simple paragraph.

The obituary was buried in the latter sections of the paper, far from a front page that was consumed with the approaching crescendo of war. Joplin's particular brand of musical wisdom had been pawned for a far more dangerous dirge. The nation was much too busy building its chorus of battle hymns to heed the diminuendo of an outdated piano professor from a previous century. I should have known then that his glossy era of rag had officially come to a close. I should have felt that in my bones and heeded the warning, but I too got caught in the throes of international turmoil.

I joined the multitude of young Negro men who joined the 369th, snared in the thrall of that national call to manhood. I marched with my fellow fodder in the great parade down 125th Street and onto the boat to France, where we climbed down into the desperate trenches of Marne, Champagne, Belleau Wood, and beyond. Even as I continued to keep Mr. Joplin's music fastened hard in my heart, it was blasted to and fro in my brain by mortars and Mausers. It was crushed by the sight of men blown to bits. It was singed by the sound of trumpets bent to war.

Between battles I witnessed Joplin's music spinning inside James Reese Europe's band like a player piano gone berserk. With each war-scorched rag, I heard what seemed like the sound of my world slowly tilting off its axis. Europe took the essence of ragtime, rolled it in the grime and blood of war, and wrung something they called *jazz* out of each instrument, smearing it all across the world's war-torn face. They were their own force; they were, as their music declared, "On Patrol in No Man's Land." Wherever we went, they sprayed the landscape raw with syncopation. They lugged their saxophones and grins into crowds of refugees and bombed out cities, and somehow made them seem to *forget*. They were heralds of a terrible, necessary transformation in the world, and they bade all who heard them to swelter that change into their bodies as they moved in its sway. In short, their music seemed to me to be a make-shift binding on a wound that did not know how to heal. A funhouse mirror, an altered lens that took all the world had known and turned it inside out, rupturing it from remembrance. A mask upon a terrible visage.

When I finally returned to Harlem from that desperate conflagration, after I'd heard the music of the war congealed with the blood of the battlefield and then set to dances—I wanted to flee from its presence. I needed to regale in the ragtime past that had been so furiously forgotten. I wanted to understand how it had been blown away, even as I was hurled, wounded and withered, from the war music's epicenter of explosion. I wanted to know better the face of original ragtime—perhaps in order to recall my own.

Upon return to the states, I rejoined my labor upon the rails. I rode, read, and listened to the world around me. I've heard the same sooty, snapping rags turned inside out all over the globe, polishing it slick as a patent leather boot that's born for more marching. Upon hearing it all over the country, I've been moved to find out what happened to the one who knew so many of those ragged secrets and had given them up so readily. The one I'd missed by moments years ago—how had he passed? How had he

10

lived? Had he truly, as so many said, lost his faculties and his mind? What had he to say about the root of his music?

Via my employer, I traveled the country in search of what Mr. Joplin was smuggling inside himself when the end came for him. And what I found is what you read here. I found a man in the mouth of turmoil, torn between the jaws of past and future. He was ripped apart by the thunder he heard in his work and the weakening squall he could make of his body onto ivory and wire. It is something both more and less than what I bargained for—but then again, I suspect that the very few who actually care about these revelations will be among those who read your publication.

Dr. Du Bois, I've read and reread your *Souls of Black Folk*. I've hummed the spirit songs that grace each chapter. I've angered with you in your thunderous declamations of injustice as I've traveled the rails in the employ of the Pullman line. I've bowed in deference to the customers, averted my gaze, toted their bags, laughed at their "humor," wiped their offal, changed their linen, fetched their liquor, warded off their women, and endured their children. I've burned myself while feeding their 20th Century furnace and stayed them on track through storm and heat. I've taken all that discipline and desperation and hauled it through the mud of France with nothing much to show for it but a broken face and a purple ribbon. But all that while, your essays have shined hard in my mind. I've dog-eared your books from Pittsburgh to Chicago to New York to Orleans and back again along a dozen railways and a quarter-million miles. You have helped to shelter me and my brotherhood in our journeys, sir. And with this small bundle of voices I hope to repay in part the debt and become, in some small sense, a fellow traveler along your course. Thank you for your time and attention to this work. I hope you find it of some use to *The Crisis*.

Sincerely,
Julius Monroe Trotter

JUBILEE BLUES

(CHORAL)

Once burst loose from human bondage,

do our songs still tow our pain like a mule?

Tell me, if we done burst loose from bondage,

do our songs still carry hurt like a mule?

They haul thundered oceans of auction blocks

homeward, pulling our lost cargo through.

If this freight of psalm should hit a rock

we're gonna do just what the old folk do.

If this load of song ever strike on rock

we gone do what we was born to do—

gone pull a whole lot harder—ain't gone stop

till all of heaven bleeds out of blue.

Every time we split our mouths to song

we'll bind the air with hallelujah's bond.

BLIND TOM PLAYS FOR CONFEDERATE TROOPS, 1863

The slave's hands dance free, unfettered, flying

across ivory, feet stomping toward

a crescendo that fills the forest pine,

reminding the Rebs what they're fighting for—

black, captive labor. Tom, slick with sweat, shows

a new trick: Back turned to his piano,

he leans like a runner about to throw

himself to freedom through forest bramble—

until he spreads his hands behind him. He

hitches fingertips to keys, hauls Dixie

slowly out of the battered upright's teeth

like a worksong dragged across cotton fields,

like a plow, weighted and dirty, ringing

with a slaver's song at master's bidding.

GENERAL JAMES BETHUNE AND
JOHN BETHUNE INTRODUCE BLIND TOM

Here he is, the Amazing Blind Tom . . .

he's pitched in darkness, exalted through sound   he's mastered sharp and flat of piano:

a slave whose head is a trunk full of song

pealing from each deft fingertip. We've found   a musical freak, a brown tornado,

a maestro who conjures three tunes at once—

a storm that brings lightning, thunder and rain   a far cry from the fields his kin slaved, he's

like a one man band. This chattel's become

filled with the light of music. His brain's   besotted with syncopation. He seems

unlocked by 88 keys to sing out

jingling with joy, the way an angel gets   blessed in the thrall of some idiot god

raptured into tongues. Tom is, beyond doubt,

winged past sorrow, each note pulled from his head   sprung from some holy, dark place that got

burnished by fate and delivered by songs

We present to you Mr. Wiggins—Ol' Blind Tom . . .

WHAT MARKED TOM?

Did a slave song at a master's bidding

mark Tom while asleep in Charity's womb?

The whole plantation would be called to sing

and dance in Master Epps' large parlor room—

after work sprung from dawn and dragged past dusk,

after children auctioned to parts unknown,

after funerals and whippings. Thus

was the whim of the patriarch. No groans

allowed, just high steppin' celebration,

grins all around, gritted or sincere.

Charity threw feet, hips, arms into motion

to please the tyrant piano. Was it here

Tom learned how music can prove the master?

While he spun in a womb of slavish laughter?

MARK TWAIN V. BLIND TOM

Some archangel,	*I'm sent from above—*
cast out of upper Heaven	*like rain on blue prayers.*
like another Satan,	*blessed with Gabriel's lost notes, I*
inhabits this coarse casket;	*can see up to God's throne, yes,*
and he comforts himself	*while he plays this soul*
and makes his prison	*of flesh free—makes me*
beautiful with	*the music of piano, the*
thoughts and	*breath and*
dreams and	*burn in the*
memories of	*stormcloud's roar from*
another time	*when sound called up,*
and another existence	*first made me whole*
that fire	*sounds like love.*
this dull clod	*weighted in my chest*
with impulses and inspirations	*—it finds freedom after*
it no more comprehends	*hurt. I hear Earth's tremble harsher*
than does the stupid worm	*—better than the soil itself. When*
the stirring of the spirit within	*land and tree sing to me, I hear*
her	*notes*
of the	*wildly*
gorgeous captive	*blooming inside—a spirit*
whose wings she	*shadows across my face,*
fetters	*breaking free*
and	*unloosed. I play the wind*
whose flight she stays	*in my blood.*

Left column is quoted from Mark Twain's letters to the San Francisco *Alta California*, August 1, 1869.

BLIND TOM PLAYS FOR A PACKED HOUSE, 1873

Tom spun wild round the room. Nervous laughter

rose from the crowd. They'd come to see a freak

of nature, one clearly gripped by the after-

world. A blind, black vessel of spiritspeak.

General Bethune, his master, took his hand

and led him to the piano. When Tom

sat down, the Wonder overtook him and

bore him down upon the keys. His song

swallowed up sunlight, spat up hurricanes,

was a rainwater baptism under

a slave's psychic hands. Was it a sound past pain,

or a hurting that knew no surrender?

The music's title seemed to beg the question:

What the Wind, Rain, and Thunder Said to Tom.

MILLIE MCKOY & CHRISTINE MCKOY RECALL MEETING BLIND TOM, 1877

Blind Tom never saw my two bodies   *He could only hear the way we were joined,*

fused at the hips. His ears saw our two   *twinned breaths colored in harmony, our blue*

bright voices blooming from one pulse. Slowly,   *reaching out through his darkness, through the void—*

he laid hands on my face, and then he knew—

but he was more curious than afraid,   *and he wasn't sad for us, thank God. He laughed,*

and even joined our chorus. We sang   *with hunger for more, wishing we could stay*

like one family praying thanks over one plate   *full of our own song. We're more than circus acts*

—our bodies' betrayals have made us a way

out of no way. We are the lucky ones   *free of the worst bondage. We're the self-owned*

—I guess. Aren't we? Folks come miles to see the true   *two-headed nightingale. Yes, we are, for sure,*

freaks: a sight and sound to amaze, to stun,   *the best duo songbirds traveling to each town*

to cause wonder at a god both kind and cruel—

It's honest work—we do it with smiles hard on our faces   *We do it knowing full well that this is our rightful place:*

to show this world the gut meaning of grace.

WHAT THE WIND, RAIN, AND THUNDER SAID TO TOM

Hear how sky opens its maw to swallow

Earth? To claim each being and blade and rock

with its spit? Become your own full sky. Own

every damn sound that struts through your ears.

Shove notes in your head till they bust out where

your eyes supposed to shine. Cast your lean

brightness across the world and folk will stare

when your hands touch piano. Bend our breath

through each fingertip uncurled and spread

upon the upright's eighty-eight pegs.

Jangle up its teeth until it can tell

our story the way you would tell your own:

the way you take darkness and make it moan.

GENERAL BETHUNE V. W.C. HANDY, 1885

Blind, half-crazy, or illiterate: this
mastermind of piano—he's a goldmine.
But Lord, he's a demon when he gets his
blood all hot. Tom's got to be feelin' high
if he's going to bring the music to life.
He'll stomp the ground and cry like a child—
and won't stop till he gets his way. He'll give strife
to anyone who plays his songs wrong. Like
when he pushed that off-tune girl off his stool
—he cursed her hard. And he's been known to strike
folk who play his songs clumsily. See, fools
get God's grace, just like a child. He just might
earn twenty thousand blessed bucks per tour
—minus management and upkeep fees, of course

Ol' Blind Tom must be some great Hoodoo
of sound workin' them keys. He's got that mojo-
magic hard. Gets some whites steamed, boils their blued
spirits 'cause he don't care 'bout 'fending folks
—he got a strong conjure on him. I hear
that he'll talk back to a white man all day—
to no-talent white women, too—I mean,
they say that blind boy got crackers all scared
and warned against messin' up his music
—no, he don't take kindly to no tone deaf
with dumb hands—he shucks 'em. But watch—Tom will
make a handsome sum for somebody, I bet—
and maybe they let him save some of that dough
—enough to send pennies to mama back home . . .

W. C. Handy met Blind Tom as a youth. General Bethune was Blind Tom's master and manager.

CHARITY ON BLIND TOM

They say Tom takes darkness and makes it moan.

I *was* his darkness. And Lawd, did I moan

when he came out to light. And moaned some more

when his eyes wouldn't catch sight. Don't

no plantation need no stumble-blind slave—

I hid him much as I could, but no way

could I keep his body's 'fliction away

from Master Epps. Blind, slow niggas don't pay

nothin' on auction block or in the field.

More trouble than they worth—better off dead,

said most white folk. I tell you—I had to kneel

deep in the dirt for that music in his head—

for General Bethune to buy us like gifts—

I had no idea Tom would make him rich.

ELIZA BETHUNE V. CHARITY WIGGINS

I know best how to take care of Tom

so that his music will flow like a river

out of desert sands. Tom's got to be calmed

with sharp words, hard hands, and denied a sliver

of patience for deceit. Truth is, I'm in dire need

of my blind boy. Our law says Tom's due

to be passed down through family, not to be

fully free. Can you imagine what he'd do?

He would be just like his colored kin,

frivolous, selfish, no-good-for-nothing

but money wasting and good time frolics.

To deliver him to his birth family,

to his mother—well, the law just won't agree

—possession is 9/10 of law, you see . . .

See, after 21 births, God gave me Tom

straight from heaven's choir. I want him back

within the bosom of family, not robbed

of all he's earned. You see, I got a lack

of help from courts. I need the 'mancipation

to start proclaimin' how all negroes was made free, not

slave to no relation of the rebel nation.

He could choose when to play and when to stop—

if he weren't bound to the Bethune's

wife who never worked at nothin'

all her inherited life. I tried to sue

and bring him home, but judges ain't listenin'

with my best interest at heart. They say

Tom will be gone from me till his dying day.

While Eliza Bethune inherited Tom after her husband's death, Tom's mother continued to sue for his return.

GENERAL BETHUNE ON BLIND TOM

I had no idea Tom would make me rich.

Blind and crazed, like a blessed-up idiot,

he'd sing bluebird songs in perfect pitch,

then bash his head against the wooden box

crib whenever his mother went to chores

in the field. He'd hop around on one leg,

bent over like a giant, pecking bird for

hours, then rattle out tunes on tin cups. I let

him stay out of compassion. Then, one day,

he heard my daughter playing piano—

Haydn, I believe. It was like a weight

fell upon him—a labor to make him whole.

My charity finally got its reward.

Who am I to deny this gift to the world?

DUET: BLIND BOONE MEETS BLIND TOM, 1889

Slave and free, we meet to burn up the day
with arpeggio and trills on our sideways harps
—we play the best way we know—it's the way
cakewalk and waltz thrum like one ripe heart
spreading through the forests, a wildfire
that cleanses and lifts me up to heaven

With fingers on keys, our hopes lifting up
in a hurricane of back and forth notes—
we storm piano's throat to feel the
full of a blood moon's glow. Our music grows
thick with smoke. I feel our Creator's touch
flying through each chord, hurling through my ears.

We turn two pianos into a choir—
music tumbling out. I want to tell him
how freedom feels, how even money can't buy
a path to song, that piano work can feed
a hungry soul. Yes, I make hard folk cry
out with joy when they hear me, when I steal
through the gut of their dreams to make them shine
like the face of dawn I've never seen—sunlight

But it seems there will never be enough
—that the hawk and eagle scream to show me
all the blue in the sky. They say that I've got
the best hunger, that I bring good news from
listening to earth's beauty. The music's brought
for them the bone-deep sound of God that hums
within themselves. This is how freedom feels—
soaring through the stars in which I reel.

BLIND TOM PLAYS ON . . .

Who am I to deny this world? This gift

of music storming through me? It howls out

my fingers when I reach into God's mouth

of piano, grabbin' fistfuls of sun with

each song. It spins me in circles, surrounds

me in starshine, mounts my head, hands, and heart

till I tell it what it wants, tell it how

we are all one wave of notes in the dark

gospel of the universe. Can't you hear

the chorus of moonlight? Can't you see

the way each note shines? It's all right here

just beneath the skin, like something I seem

to remember—the sound of my mother crying

while her hands danced across me—free, flying . . .

BLIND TOM: ONE BODY, TWO GRAVES

BROOKLYN/GEORGIA

Here I lie, Blind Tom: Piano Man. I'm free

here in Brooklyn soil, I'm 'mancipated—   like so much Georgia dust; I rest quiet—

like lightnin' bugs ghostin' up night. And now I can see—

at last! I watch each piano's breath bated   beneath pinetop and cedar. I feel God's riot

beneath each finger that seeks to strike a key

in the key of wonder. I conjure a claim   of birdsongs blended from each season's sun

rooted deep in black muscle memory

that's set slaves almost free, that carved its name   scrawling across each heart, the music's brunt

ringing like a bell, like an open wound

thick as thunder through city summer air—   shimmering all over the country's soul—

from mouths that bend flattened dreams into tune—

I'm nowhere at all, but sing everywhere—   I dance inside each holla and whole note—

Let me introduce to those who ain't heard me:

Here I am, Blind Tom: Piano Man. Free.

Blind Tom was buried first in Brooklyn's Evergreen Cemetery, and then allegedly moved by the Bethune family to Columbus, GA. However, records in Brooklyn indicate the body was never moved. There are headstones in both states for Blind Tom.

JUBILEE: ISAAC DICKERSON (1852–1900)

We boil the air with hallelujah's balm

'cause each of us got a story to yell

out in song. Mine starts with my lonesome

crying in the dark. Pa'd whispered: *They gone sell*

me in the morning, son. By five years old,

I was orphaned. By nine, it was war.

I got conscripted by the Rebs. They told

me Yanks weren't fit to live. That they fought for

raping and pillaging nigger skin. That

free will was just a trap. A deck of cards

stacked against black. Well, now I full see what

they ain't want me to believe. It's a far

sight better than those chains that held us hostage—

we burned down *Dixie*'s shack with our palace of freed voice.

DELLA MARIE JENKINS, RN, NEW YORK, NY: SEPT. 19, 1924

SUBMITTED TO *THE CRISIS* BY JULIUS MONROE TROTTER

Mrs. Della Jenkins, who cared for Mr. Joplin in his final days, agreed to share her memories of that time. We met at the Harlem offices of the Universal Negro Improvement Association near 125th and Lenox.

I only know what I saw up close when I tended to Mr. Joplin, but I'll share what I have.

Thank you, ma'am.

How did you find out I was his nurse?

The hospital told me you were in charge of his ward during his last days.

You got a lot of gumption. You get that in the war? You one of the 369, am I right?

That's true, ma'am. But that gumption you talk about is mostly just plain curiosity.

Curiosity. That's a double-edged sword. Did that curiosity get you your wound?

If you want to call being at the wrong end of a Mauser curiosity, I guess so, ma'am.

Well, I hope they at least mustered you out with recognition. That's more than they did for us nurses.

I made out okay, ma'am.

You got a medal, then?

Yes, ma'am. Don't travel with it, though. Sent it back home to my people.

That's advisable.

Yes, it is.

I've seen what happens to you Hellfighters when you come home with your medals all showing out on your chests. Best to keep 'em hidden. 'Cause later on I'd see those same medals hanging from trees when y'all try to wear them in public.

I've seen that too, Mrs. Jenkins.

Besides, you got your medal with that patchwork face of yours. That is excellent craftsmanship there, friend. They got your shade just right. You don't notice until you're right up close. I've seen the operations, and they don't always work out so well. This was most probably the best choice.

Well, the doctors in France were generous. And they didn't care about my color. It took me a while, but I realize now that I'm a . . . lucky one.

Yes, you are. Before I joined the Black Cross, I saw wounds like yours on the soldiers we tended to in the Red Cross. Those boys got the American doctors, but they weren't near as good as those French. Not at this kind of work.

Vive la France! They had a lot of practice.

The French. I heard the stories about all those battles, how they would only let y'all fight with the French—from the Marne to Verdun and back. Bet you saw a lot of the country, huh?

I saw my fair share. And then, it was hospital.

Yes, of course. Well, we couldn't tend to the white soldiers at Camp Grant in Illinois. We could only tend the German POWs and the colored boys. And most times, we were obliged to serve the Germans first. Germans was right 'fraid of y'all that's for sure. Called you Black Devils and all. Said y'all fought like there was no turning back.

Well, there wasn't. The brass made sure of that.

(*Laughs*) God bless 'em for that, son. All of you. Going over there looking for something like manhood. Coming back with something to carry in your hand that looked like respect. A cross or a Purple Heart or a ribbon to prove we'll bleed just as hard as any white man for this country. As if we ain't proved that already.

Thank you, ma'am.

31

But you listen close: ain't enough medals or ribbons in the world to prove Negro worth to the white man. That war proved that. And now it's a new day. "The first dying that is to be done by the black man in the future will be done to make himself free. And then when we are finished, *if* we have any charity to bestow, we *may* die for the white man." You know who said that?

No ma'am.

The Honorable Marcus M. Garvey, my brother. They locked him away, but they can't lock down the truth. And the truth is with the Negro and his destiny. And that destiny is to never take the white man's orders again.

Well, this soldier's soldiering days are done, ma'am. And all I know is that whatever happened over there was a loss of more than people, but ideas. Like the music of Joplin.

The music of Joplin, huh? You say he was a ragtime man . . . You know that tune *Every Race Has a Flag but the Coon*?

How could I not? That's one of those songs white folks whistle and hum whenever they want to get a rise out of us.

That sounds like the kind of music maybe needs to get lost. Especially now, seeing as how the Negro has made his very own flag: the red, black, and green banner of the United Negro Improvement Association. Some ideas, like those coon songs, *need* to go away. Did this Joplin fellow write that one?

No ma'am. That was some white folks' coon song. Not Joplin. He wrote ragtime. Strictly ragtime.

But he did write some of them coon songs, didn't he?

Well, he might've written one or two.

And you wondering why folk ain't listening to ragtime no more?

Well, there's a . . .

No need to explain. All the music in the world ain't gonna change one fact. No matter it's ragtime or spirituals or jazz, nothing short of unification and nationhood gonna get us a single shred of respect and power out this world.

I believe Mr. Joplin was making power out of his music.

e I ran across him all that power was mostly nothing but a string

y ol' hospital air. Wasn't enough to save him or nobody else in the

about it? How he spent his last days?

yphilis took him down. Slow. Slow way to go. Must've had it for

hospital he was barely moving. You know, funny thing is I didn't

weeks after he came there. He didn't play much at all while I

wasn't much to be done by that point but dose him up and let him

ay much. Moved very little, except when I would hold him up for

les on the bedside table. I would be wiping him down while he

slow motion and stiff, all herky jerky like a rusted up gadget. So

ow much of whoever came to visit, but knew how to find middle

is head nobody else could hear. Course, that might've been sick-

music stuck all up in his hands, him trying to work it all out before

Like I said, he didn't play much, except when he was all feeble finger-twitching on the air, or on the table, or on the wall, or on his stretched out legs. But one last time he played the real piano in the great room, I think it had been months since he touched a key. Really wasn't supposed to have him down there, as he was terminal care and all. But did it matter? That's what I thought anyway. Man about to pass on over, he might as well have one last play. Wheeled him down there a few days before he passed, let him sit in a wheelchair stacked up on pillows. Didn't do nothing for such a long time, nothing but stare at the keys, his eyes all empty like broken pails. But then he moved. A little. It was like watching raw sap coming out a tree, he was moving so slow—and when he hit that first note, it barely made a sound. By the end, he wasn't nothing but a tremble.

What did he play?

Well now, I must confess that I don't know all of those songs. Most I know is how he played, what it was sounding like. So, at first he played pretty good, you know—like the kind of good you want to tell somebody about just right before you doze off. The kind of notes that come strong at first and then fade to the next till you wonder where you began and they end at. Then other times . . .

He'd make me want to just look away. He'd look up from the keys and through . . . through me, through the brick and mortar ward, through Manhattan, like he was looking out a window wondering whether to jump, half blind one second, sway headed like a newborn the next. And when he played like that, it was . . . well . . . old timey one minute, then lovely terrible. Like he had another life in the music, but he couldn't get it all the way out to save him in this one. Or like he was playing another language on the keys, begging us to hear it with him. And then sometimes playing all slow like he wanted us to learn every note. Then other times he'd be frantic, digging through them black and whites like he was lookin for something he'd lost, what was left of himself.

Was it ragtime?

Yes sir, it was ragtime alright . . . And then it was just plain raggedy. All stitched together; loose in some parts and painful tight in others. Heard a cakewalk in there, but then the walk started to lean too hard and got drunk off its own sway. Heard some spirituals: *Nearer My God to Thee*, *Most Done Toiling Here*, but they wore too much pride to be prayerful. Heard a hint of that new blue music, but he let the keys sing too free to be truly sorrowed. It was a true mix up, boy, I'm tellin you. Didn't know rightly how to feel after he stopped, wasn't no way to know whether a man should just take his hat off his head or throw it up in the air, whether a woman should put her hands together over and over or just hold them up to her mouth with a silent prayer. So we all just sat there and watched. Silent. The sick, the dying, the nurses. We watched him crawl all over that keyboard like a beggar in the gutter and a king on the sauce. Watched him leave half his life spread across the keys till he left himself half-dead.

That ragtime man, maybe he knew something we didn't know, though. I could've swore when he was playing that last tune in the great room, that he was just . . . *glowing* . . . with something I ain't never seen before. Almost like he was listening to it and smilin deep inside himself.

How long did he play?

(*Pause*) What's time got to do with it? (*Laughter, slight*) . . . Long enough, son. Long enough.

JUBILEE: ELIZA WALKER (1857–?)

Ma's singing would make our slave shack a palace.

In the night's soft pitch, her voice would outshine

any moon—moaning with a wanting way

that broke winter's hold to warm us. Oh yes . . . I

can still feel her woolen hum. 'Specially when

trekking 'cross country singing Jubilee.

Like how she sang when daddy's last payment

bought us free. He'd earned cash by keeping the freeze

of winter stored in summer. *It turns out*

Nigger ice gets just as froze as Whites'! he'd

declare. We rose from slave house to icehouse

thanks to Southern heat. See, I've got daddy's cool, steeled

by mama's blazing hymns. When we sing, I feel

them songs getting freed up from tangled cane fields.

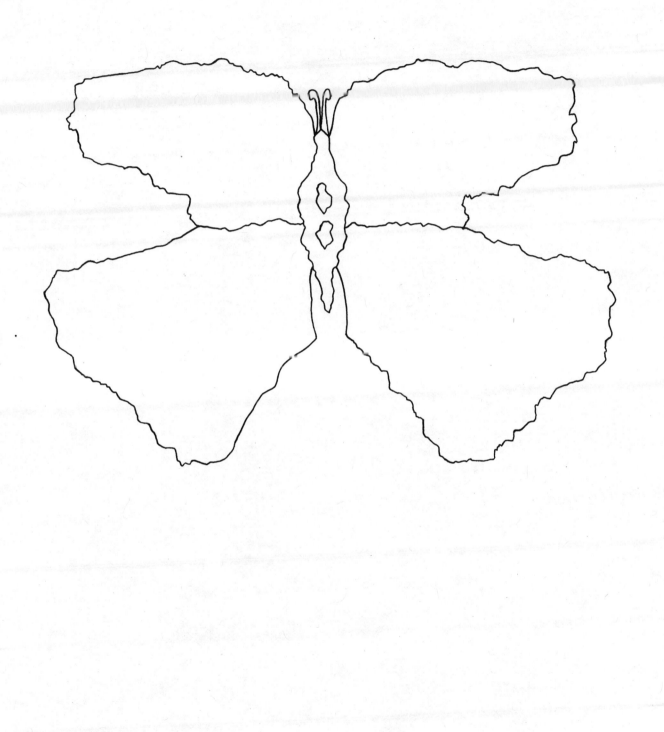

WE are, indeed, a strange people, justly regarded both by scientific and ordinary eyes as the greatest natural curiosities the world has ever had sent upon its surface.

MILLIE AND CHRISTINE MCKOY

We've mended two songs into one dark skin

bleeding soprano into contralto

—we're fused in blood and body—from one thrummed stem

budding twin blooms of song. We're a doubled rose

descended from raw carnage of the South

bursting open our freedom. We sing past rage

grown from hard labor that made our mother shout,

spent with awe. We hymn to pay soft homage

to the worksong's aria. It leaves us

soaked in history like our father's sweat

borne of and beyond the flesh: we are just

two women singing truths we can't forget

from plantation to grave. Lord, here we are,

freed twin sisters who've hauled our voices far . . .

We ride the wake of each other's rhythm

beating our hearts' syncopated tempo

with a music all our own. With our mouths

seeped in the glow of hand-me-down courage

drenched in spiritual a cappellas,

flowing soul from bone through skin. We pay debts

from broken chattel to circus stars,

we sing straight from this nation's barbwired heart . . .

We have been examined most scrutinizingly by too many

medical men to be regarded as humbugs by any one.

MILLIE-CHRISTINE: ON DISPLAY

We count the blessings of our doubled shell

with each breath. We prove we've endured faith's storm   every time we rise to face the crowd's face—

as we pay our dues. We've proven ourselves

to those who doubt our form. We have performed   on display. We've been richly, rudely paid

for science. We've been taken town to town

   —been photographed half-nude, verified   to prove veracity. They've scanned each side

like prize bovine: We've been pawed up and down—

from my twin's navel to between her thighs   and then back up, staring into my eyes—

each sawbone has searched us from spine to loin—

We've been probed, prodded, and roughly exammed—   from backbone to backbone, from hip to hip

our wondrous oneness exists. We're conjoined.

and we've lists of doctors who understand   our miracle is real. Hear and see this:

We're not frauds, but born of providence:

God mended two souls into one dark skin.

Taking advantage of the absence of our kind master and

guardian, the man absolutely kidnapped us, stole us from

our mother, and bore us far away from friends, kindred,

or any one who had a right to feel an interest in us.

MILLIE-CHRISTINE ARE KIDNAPPED

Straight from America's barbwired heart

we'd been rented and sold, then snatched! Taken   like doubled dark treasures; entertainment

at the age of three—we'd been kidnapped afar—

like contraband, we'd been shipped to Britain,   imported by a scallywag agent—

we'd been stolen from mother and master. Absconded,

we'd been smuggled to freedom's soil. And yes,   from slavery we'd slipped into liberty—

the thief's greed had set us free! Although bonded,

though we'd missed family, were we not blessed?   because of our great popularity

we'd earned a London court's sympathy, and thus,

we went back to bondage in mother's arms.   we sailed back to our Carolina home.

We returned to a master we could trust—

choosing between homeland and untold harms,   torn 'tween family or freedom's unknowns

our mother left England and went back South—

Straight into Dixie's rebellious mouth

We wished to be viewed as something entirely

void of humbug—a living curiosity—not a sham

gotten up to impose upon and deceive the people.

MILLIE-CHRISTINE'S LOVE STORY

Here—this is our story I want you to hear—

our own duet. Listen to how we're bound   in unison. Listen to the grace we have

—one body crooning two notes. By God, we're

like sympathetic strings. Each sung sound   ringing within me and my other half;

airborne, shook and shimmering through my head,

with Christine's voice at my side. I have sung   with Millie's embracing contrapuntal,

in a way very few could comprehend—

with souls ablaze. This is how I know love—   so you can see my life is brimmed. It's full—

with every breath we've got. I'm filled completely,

the way any other human would love.   I live each day like I won't see its night,

I love my song and dance and family—

the way you love your own blood. Twice as much.   I've double the cause to celebrate life.

I love this burden that we've been given—

to ride the shared wake of one blood's rhythm . . .

We are indeed a strange freak of Nature, and

upon the success of our exhibition does our

happiness and the well doing of others depend.

MILLIE-CHRISTINE BUY LAND

We're freed twin sisters who've hauled our voices far . . .

We melodize worldwide. More than just freaks,   we're certified global phenomena:

Wir singen in drei Sprachen und machen es schwarz!

Nous avons chanté le français à Paris!   We've sung hymns before Queen Victoria!

We speak more than one tongue. Wherever we roam

we've made our wealth. For gratification,   we earn respect. We give solid proof that

this gift's pure gold! While we travel the road,

we pay mortgage on our old plantation—   the Lord provides for us. We make greenbacks—

with dimes hoarded by pinching francs and pounds

for our folks. Thus, we buy liberation   from each gawking crowd. Meanwhile, dollars stack—

against servitude. We sing freedombound

—and we know the cost. We've overcome   from the root of our guts. We give back

with duets all mingled up to heaven

—we've bought land that once enslaved our parents . . .

MCKOY TWINS
SYNCOPATED STAR

JUBILEE: BEN HOLMES (1846–1875)

I'd hear these songs borne raw from cane fields,

tangled up in the work of the dirt with

the hurting of the lash. Now, I was real

lucky. I was a tailor's 'prentice.

But then I got sold to a slave trader.

Went from threading needle to squalid slave pen,

grubbin' old cow's head and grits . . . till later

on, someone slipped me that Proclamation

of Lincoln's. 'Long came overdue freedom . . .

next comes book learnin'. We've traveled hard,

each tongue spinning spirituals into tens and ones

to buy Fisk its spellers and bricks. Here we are,

each voice shimmerin' like ol' North Star's rapture . . .

we've come far by strapping lungs to scripture.

SAM PATTERSON, HARLEM, NY: DEC. 12, 1924

An accomplished ragtime pianist himself, Sam Patterson was quite close to Joplin throughout his Missouri days and on until his death in 1917. I interviewed Mr. Patterson in Manhattan at the Harlem YMCA, during one of his travels to New York.

Thank you for your time, Mr. Patterson. I understand you were rather close to Mr. Joplin.

Yes, you could say that. Knocked around together for years. But I am curious . . . what is it got you so bent on knowing Joplin's story?

Well sir, his tunes . . . they have given me great comfort in times of need. They saved me in times of voracious grief. They help me remember who I am. Where I'm from. Who I was.

Yes. The music will do that—take pain and pour it someplace else for a while.

I believe that his story is higher . . . deeper than the sound of his music. If people knew the sheer will that was put into each note, they might know better how those tunes, that music, let this country talk itself through its own ugliness. I want to uncover the details of his process. I've been talking to the people who knew him most intimately, the ones best able to carry his memory forward. So here I am, putting his story together so I can better know . . . ours. I'm hoping you will help me, sir.

I see. (*Laughs*)

You got high expectations, you know that? You don't always get the story you want. It don't always show the way to where you think you're going to. And then too, it don't change nothing if it's the past. And ain't nothing sound more like the past these days than some old ragtime tunes. Some things you just can't get back.

I'm here for the story as it happened. That's all I need, Mr. Patterson.

Well. You seem to know a thing or two about loss. How the world don't slow itself one step. Whole world seems sold on racing away from whatever it's ever been. Hooked on leaving its past behind without a trace. Especially after war.

ntinent a double dose of darkie believed to be one of a kind and probably the last of its kind born from an ordinary Negro

 of one they walk and they talk they sing and they dance they'll astound and amaze as they attract your gaze they'll be a

 bodies (or is it body?) it's a mystery of language and philosophy decide for yourself is it them or is it she is it me or is it

 either fallen from heaven or risen from hell only they know the answer and it's here for sale here for a low low price as

nder of the universe for a tiny portion of what's in your purse a money back guarantee if you can verify that you've seen

 their minds employed independently watch one twin smile while the other twin frowns examine between the creases of

urgeons and see the wonders of science at work put your fingers across their skin and try to figure where one ends and

 edges and follow the lines of each sister where their hips combine and examine for yourself the veracity of our claims

 man's burden you will certainly not regret the opportunity to lay your eyes on our century's greatest surprise step right

 humanity laid bare for you to read nature's dark strange story in their twin bodies step right up . . .

We count the blessings of our doubled shell

with each breath. We prove we've endured faith's storm   every time we rise to face the crowd's face—

as we pay our dues. We've proven ourselves

to those who doubt our form. We have performed   on display. We've been richly, rudely paid

for science. We've been taken town to town

—been photographed half-nude, verified   to prove veracity. They've scanned each side

like prize bovine: We've been pawed up and down—

from my twin's navel to between her thighs   and then back up, staring into my eyes—

each sawbone has searched us from spine to loin—

We've been probed, prodded, and roughly exammed—   from backbone to backbone, from hip to hip

our wondrous oneness exists. We're conjoined.

and we've lists of doctors who understand   our miracle is real. Hear and see this:

We're not frauds, but born of providence:

God mended two souls into one dark skin.

We've mended two songs into one dark skin

bleeding soprano into contralto

—we're fused in blood and

budding twin blooms o

descended from raw carnage of the South

bursting open our freedom. We sing past rage

grown from hard labor

spent with awe. We

to the worksong's aria. It leaves us

soaked in history like our father's sweat

borne of and beyor

two women singin

from plantation to grave. Lord, here we are,

freed twin sisters who've hauled our voices far . . .

We're freed twin sisters who've hauled our voices far . . .

We melodize worldwide. More than just freaks,   we're certified global phenomena:

Wir singen in drei Sprachen und machen es schwarz!

Nous avons chanté le français à Paris!   We've sung hymns before Queen Victoria!

We speak more than one tongue. Wherever we roam

we've made our wealth. For gratification,   we earn respect. We give solid proof that

this gift's pure gold! While we travel the road,

we pay mortgage on our old plantation—   the Lord provides for us. We make greenbacks—

with dimes hoarded by pinching francs and pounds

for our folks. Thus, we buy liberation   from each gawking crowd. Meanwhile, dollars stack—

against servitude. We sing freedombound

—and we know the cost. We've overcome   from the root of our guts. We give back

with duets all mingled up to heaven

—we've bought land that once enslaved our parents . . .

Here—this is our story I want you to hear—
our own duet. Listen to how we're bound   in unison. Listen to the grace we have
—one body crooning two notes. By God, we're
like sympathetic strings. Each sung sound   ringing within me and my other half;
airborne, shook and shimmering through my head,
with Christine's voice at my side. I have sung   with Millie's embracing contrapuntal,
in a way very few could comprehend—
with souls ablaze. This is how I know love—   so you can see my life is brimmed. It's full—
with every breath we've got. I'm filled completely,
the way any other human would love.   I live each day like I won't see its night,
I love my song and dance and family—
the way you love your own blood. Twice as much.   I've double the cause to celebrate life.
I love this burden that we've been given—
to ride the shared wake of one blood's rhythm . . .

We ride the wake of each other's rhythm
beating our hearts' syncopated tempo
body—from one thrummed stem
song. We're a doubled rose
with a music all our own. With our mouths
seeped in the glow of hand-me-down courage
that made our mother shout,
hymn to pay soft homage
drenched in spiritual a cappellas,
flowing soul from bone through skin. We pay debts
d the flesh: we are just
truths we can't forget
from broken chattel to circus stars,
we sing straight from this nation's barbwired heart . . .

Straight from America's barbwired heart
we'd been rented and sold, then snatched! Taken   like doubled dark treasures; entertainment
at the age of three—we'd been kidnapped afar—
like contraband, we'd been shipped to Britain,   imported by a scallywag agent—
we'd been stolen from mother and master. Absconded,
we'd been smuggled to freedom's soil. And yes,   from slavery we'd slipped into liberty—
the thief's greed had set us free! Although bonded,
though we'd missed family, were we not blessed?   because of our great popularity
we'd earned a London court's sympathy, and thus,
we went back to bondage in mother's arms.   we sailed back to our Carolina home.
We returned to a master we could trust—
choosing between homeland and untold harms,   torn 'tween family or freedom's unknowns
our mother left England and went back South—
Straight into Dixie's rebellious mouth

... step right up ladies and gents boys and gals and see the two headed nightingale the McKoy Twins never before seen on this cc

mother who gave 200% profits to her master with 10,000,000 to 1 odds of labor more than she bargained for got two for the price

sight you'll never forget at a price you'll never regret just a small fee to see their indelible story written all over their doubled up

we you can decide for yourself for just a small fee inspect the body of these urchin darkies the story that their bodies tell is one

you look them up and down and side to side and backwards and forwards then you can decide whether or not you've seen a wo

another pair of twins with this mixed up story of their limbs with their backs conjoined but their hearts enjoying life separately

their bodies for the crease between the self and the other the figured and disfigured step right up step right up physicians and s

the other begins how darkness stretches across two bodies at the same time how two negresses share the same spine fondle th

before we put them on the stage of your town the syncopated brown sisters from Carolina the double blessed twice cursed whit

up fine people examine her side to side and backwards and forwards and diagonally you can see the conjoined twins' entwined

That's true, sir.

I see that you've seen your share.

I have, sir. With the 369th.

Took a chunk out of you, huh?

Yes sir. Belleau Wood.

Damn. You ain't that one that won the Croix de Guerre, are you?

No, sir. Just one that got a bit . . . rearranged.

Well, then. Let me pour us a toast . . . Tell me. What story you want to hear? What you need to know?

I want to know about his unpublished work. You helped Mr. Joplin write his final scores?

Well, I was with him. I was in that room with him for days—weeks. He was pressing up on them keys like he was trying to look into a mirror and find his own face. Blood gone almost all the way bad by then.

Syphilis?

Yeah. That bad blooded dog. It bit him up and spat him out—left nothing but dry bones and a crop of scattered nerves—just enough for him to try and stutter out some last scraps of sound. It was rough, boy. Rough.

Did he get much done?

Well, in a seeming sort of way. Problem was, he couldn't hardly start one rag before he would get up and go to the next. Was all broiled up in each one—start one sounding like morning, get halfway through, and end up switching to some chords that left a midnight taste in your mouth. Start another that blew through your bones like a winter frost, then he'd take a break and come back burning up them keys like August in a cotton field.

Did he finish any of those compositions?

Can't tell you. Might have—but most of what he did finish he ended up callin child's play. But they weren't any child's play, I'll tell you that. Not any child I ever met. I know 'cause I heard him play it all together one time, just before he lit that match.

You mean that he played the whole thing at once? As one piece?

The whole thing. Took all them raggedy pieces and tied 'em all together with a loose string of phrases all syncopated up like a gold pocket watch. A dozen dozen little song parts ticking away, all coiled up spitting and spinning. Times falling away and then coming together at the last minute . . . goodness.

Did it have a name?

Can't say it did. Only saw him play it that one night. And everything he was working on was changing titles all the time, anyway. One hour it'd be the *If Rag*, then turn around and it'd be *Lost Boy*. Next hour, it'd be the *Magnetic Rag. Remember Me. Tremble Hand. Hallelujah. Bad Blood. Palms Down. Syncopated Glories. Morning Burl*. Seem like they was all getting born up at once—everything he'd had me writing down for all those days and nights. I couldn't rightly say that all of it was nice sounding. But some of it stuck to me so hard until I could never shake it off. Or maybe it was the way he was playing it—like he was staring down a well. And then sometimes he'd just stop and look at his palms, like he'd brung up a last drink of water. Then he'd just splash it all over that piano.

But I can still hear parts of it in my head. (*Plays*)

That was some good stuff right there. 'Cept he'd played it all stiffed up, bar by bar, most the time. Till that one last night.

Were you there that night?

I was there. Well, naw I wasn't there. I was supposed to be. See, he had just played that thing. Had played it all out, till there wasn't no more. He was sweating and heaving at the end like he'd been running for everything he'd ever lost. I remember once he looked up like he'd found some secret in the music, and then he did something he'd rarely do—he sang a little with the tune, like *I'm in the wind, baby. I'm in the wind, darling*. He was just twirling them keys all around, you know. Just twinkling up those high notes with big bashes of bass. Then too, I remember there was this one part in the music where he sounded like he'd wandered somewhere deep in the notes and couldn't find a way back. Well, he found his way back alright. But he just wasn't the same no more.

What happened? How was he different?

Well, let me see . . . You ever have someone seem all never-beaten all their life, so never-beaten till it's like they was never weak? So strong till the day you come to know how weak they are—that's when you see how you never knew their strength? Well, I had been knowing him for days, weeks, years. All the time knowing 'bout his strength—knowing he would be hitting those keys to the end, even when he was out of it, he'd walk out with his head up. He'd seen worse. Lot worse.

See, sometimes he'd be out on the road, playing his set—everything that had got his name on it, his bread and butter. He'd be up there playin it all grand and professor-like, kinda stilted up and slowed down so that the audience could hear every note shimmering in its own museum. He'd love each rag like it was the children he never got to see grow up—he'd be keepin them all orderly and polite, straining up their voices—not so much as they'd break, but enough to hear them bend up a little into hope, no matter how sad they might be. But never rushin nowhere. Folks was all okay with that back when he first started playin that *Maple Leaf* and such.

But it changed. He thought putting those pieces on paper would help hold them the way he heard them—make them stay proper and well behaved.

I imagine he was quite eager to get his work published in order to get compensated.

Yeah, he was glad to see it out in the world. See, he wanted to leave his sound behind him . . . but see, it didn't work out quite exactly like that. Once those rags were on paper, every ten-fingered bowler-wearing stud would put his hands all over those tunes. Walk them slow at first, till they learned all their ins and outs. They was polite with them tunes, till they figured out how to roll 'em out a little faster, and then make 'em strut and swagger more with each stride. Next thing you know, they was cakewalking them rags up and down that keyboard like a pimp in the tenderloin. Their fingers would work 'em more faster, more prettier than they was supposed to be—all slicked up and leaned back and sideways steppin—hustled up and tricked out like something illegal, ill tempered and ill-begotten gained.

And started to be like every time he went to a new town, there'd be some light-fingered hustler out to bootstrap himself up, using Scott like a ladder. Come up onstage after Scott all friendly, then play his pieces all to pieces. I mean snapping those rags with a shoeshine boy's spit and polish, trying to make the best tip of the week by showing the master how to work his own business. He'd say in his polite little professor tone, "Very nice, but too fast, friend!" and they'd just laugh. He would laugh with them a little through his frown, too—because what else could he do?

And what's make it worse is that Scott couldn't keep up with 'em. That ol' dog syphilis had him by the throat, and had gnawed up almost everything he could do with his hands . . . and every year it got worse, till he would come into town and some folks would think he must've been a faker, askin how could the great rag man be all dusted up and unpolished like that? This be Scott Joplin? *This?*

But he never stopped, brother. Never stopped. Would always shake it off, even though you knew he'd been shook. Always had a plan—an opera, a show . . .

Like Treemonisha*, right? Isn't that what kept him going?*

Yeah, trying to get that opera up and runnin kept him going for a long time. Years, maybe. But everybody got limits. And that night, he knew he'd just . . . run out of time. He'd played that patchworked blanket of rags for hours and hours that night, all up and down the fingerboard till the air was about beat out the room. And he was breathless. When he looked up you could see there weren't that many breaths left for him here on this earth, and when I saw his face . . . boy, I just had to . . .

I had to walk away for a while. I went out that door. Got the night air. Cleaned myself off with a walk beneath the streetlights.

So . . . you left the building . . .

Yeah. Only left about twenty minutes or so, walking round the block. Came back and there was a glowing off the roof of the building. Ran up all them stairs, thinking the building was on fire, maybe one of them johns had dropped a cigar on the roof. Got there to see him standing next to this big old metal trash can, all blazed up with his songs. He must've put some kerosene on them 'cause they was blazed up pretty high and hot—I could feel the heat off those rags—damn, all them beautiful rags—could feel the heat from ten feet away. And I could see Scott on the other side. His face all lit up, his hands trembling and holding one last stash of scribbled up music.

You can't stop something you know is gonna happen anyway. And then, you still gotta try. And I did. I tried to fix my mouth to talk at him, talk him down from all that mischief the sickness had put up in his brain. But what could I say? All the things you would say in the same situation. *Don't do it, Scott— your voice on paper, your work, think of your bloodline of sound all burning up, man . . . Who gone show them, man? People need to know . . .*

You know what he said?

What did he say?

It was almost like he knew it was coming. This giant hand of wind came right over us from the river. And he threw them rags all up in the air and into the palm of that hand, and it made a fist and smeared his music all over New York. All them notes all scattered over Manhattan like so many raindrops. All them notes burning up in smoke.

What'd he say? *It's all in the wind, Sam. It's all in the wind.*

JUBILEE: MINNIE TATE (1857–?)

Here we are, strapping voice to scripture

so the world might love Black breaths livin' free.

Now, I've never been a slave, but I'm sure

close enough to have felt its searing ways. See,

mother was freed when she was a girl. Went

to school with whites—chose to school me at home.

When she sent me to Fisk, she never meant

for me to roam with a choir on the road.

But I've learned things here I might've never

known. Like the time a train station mob

of mad whites swarmed. We didn't know whether

we'd live or be killed . . . so, we just did our job:

hushed them to shame by hymning on Divine Will

till they wept like 'Zekiel under that blazin' wheel.

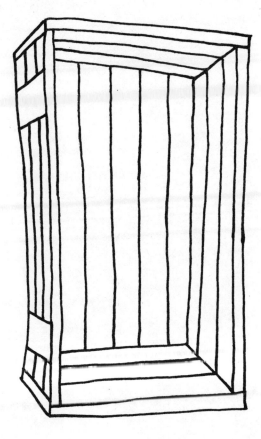

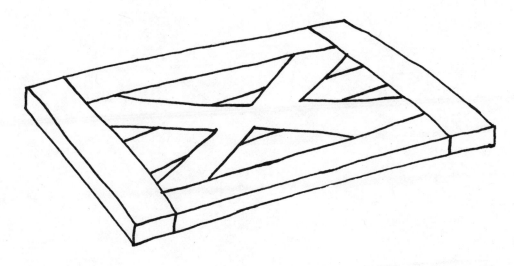

INTRODUCING

MIRROR OF
SLAVERY/MIRROR
CHICANERY

The Freed Songs of Berryman/Brown

In which the escaped slave and travelling mesmerist Mr. Henry "Box" Brown blackens the voice of poet Mr. John Berryman's "Henry" from The Dream Songs and liberates him(self) from literary bondage!

* * * *

A coloured gentleman, Mr. H. B. Brown, purposes to visit your village for the purpose of exhibiting his splendid Panorama, or Mirror of Slavery. I have had the pleasure of seeing it, and . . . in my opinion, it is almost, if not quite, a perfect fac simile of the workings of that horrible and fiendish system.

REV. JUSTIN SPAULDING of Dover, New Hampshire, July 12, 1850

* * * *

Dere was an old Nigga, dey call'd him Uncle Ned—
He's dead long ago, long ago!
He had no wool on de top ob his head—
De place whar de wool ought to grow.

STEPHEN FOSTER, "Ol' Uncle Ned," 1848

71

Here you see a man by the name of Henry Brown
Run away from the South to the North
Which he would not have done but they stole all his rights
But they'll never do the like again . . .

HENRY BROWN, "Song Composed on His Escape From Slavery"
(sung to the air of "Ol' Uncle Ned"), 1849

* * * *

PRE/FACE
BERRYMAN/BROWN

The poem then,	Let me say,
whatever its wide cast of characters,	despite loss . . . I won my life. This story—
is essentially about	how a slave steals back his skin:
an imaginary character	smuggles loose like I did. It lives on,
(not the poet,	but through words—and
not me)	free. I'm
named Henry,	"Box" Brown. Ain't
a white American	masking my truth: one day,
in early middle age,	I delivered myself.
sometimes	I ache
in	my
blackface,	love for
who has suffered	. . . those left behind.
an irreversible loss	. . . Berryman can't talk for them,
and talks about himself . . .	can't tell my tale at all.

Italicized text excerpted from John Berryman's introductory note to *The Dream Songs*.

FREEDSONG: DREAM GONE

O dear, I thought, shall my wife and children no more greet
my sight with their cheerful looks and happy smiles!
NARRATIVE OF THE LIFE OF HENRY BOX BROWN

Let's bless Henry. Treated like a rat,

with hand of a slaver 'pon his head

from his beginning.

Henry was not a coward, much.

He never deserted anything; but yes,

he struck out when family went thinning.

Some didn't see Henry as human being.

Let's interrogate that.

. . . He slaved, all day.

Yet, he's a human American man.

And blue. His back was breaking.

His mask was aching. Stunned and diminished, he mapped escape.

Their God? Henry's enemy. Fear, its business. Wild,

white business caused Henry's tears

at auctioning.

He could feel its terror in his bones

as he looked at an empty sky

that stripped him of family.

FROM DREAM SONG 13

FREEDSONG: DREAM DAWN

Thus passed my child from my presence . . . I could only say, farewell, and leave it to pass in its chains
while I looked for the approach of another gang in which my wife was also loaded with chains.

NARRATIVE OF THE LIFE OF HENRY BOX BROWN

There sat down, hard, a thing upon Henry's heart
so heavy, if he had a hundred years
& more, & weeping, sleepless, in all that time
Henry would not make good.
Starts again always in Henry's fears
a brittle loss somewhere. His old love, his wife.

And there is a smothered thing he has in mind
like a grave comedy's fate. A thousand years
would fail to blur her still profile in the dusk. Ghastly,
with closed eyes, he pretends she's nigh.
All his cells say: too late. Then there are his tears,
sinking.

But never did Henry, as some thought he should,
end a master and hack their body up
and hide the pieces where they wouldn't be found.
He knows he wanted to. So, he went gone. He went missing.
Often he reckons, on the dawn, his love.
Her body is ever missing.

FROM DREAM SONG 29

FREEDSONG: OF 1850*

. . . it is not safe for us to stay about here . . . we have made arrangements to go to England . . .

H. B. BROWN, LTR. TO GERIT SMITH, 1850

Industrious, affable, having brain on fire,

Henry did vex the South. Slavers raked up

the world, making

getting home-free harder on freedmen. Tired

fugitives were lashed; languished. Anguished hearts accrued

on what once had been

free splendor of the North. H's blues became

dire. His heart stuffed and he failed to smile,

Catching freemen is

now law! he cussed. Forgoing brief acclaim,

bracing his pride, he went onward. He smiled

each mile to Old London.

Still free and lucky, Henry made a roar

overseas. Presses kept on thundering:

his mystery was cool

fire! H. "Box" Brown: His brutal story bore

rave reviews. He burst on the scene

with great aplomb.

FROM DREAM SONG 58

*Fugitive Slave Act passed, allowing slavers to kidnap escaped slaves in Northern states.

FREEDSONG: DREAM STRONG

Mr. H. Box Brown, The King of All Mesmerisers

HANDBILL, 1864

Spellbound held subtle Henry all his foll-
owers with the racket of his sales pitch:
his painted signs, his slave panoramas
and mesmerism. More, then less, he was beloved
for his day. His act was more and more
revenging . . . still, they paid him.

He was not so tied up in befriending
his critics. Famous Henry'd railed on Southern
slavers that mauled
deeply in his mother country. So
he'd plied his heart and brains and wail. He was
cuffed with love for his freedom.

Once, he'd preached to them—all open-mouthed.
Prayed that they'd learn. Then, war's monsoon spread
its blood through and through
the States. Freedom won. So, H. began
in his accustomed way toward the place he'd left.
Across the waters, he came.

FROM DREAM SONG 71

83

FREEDSONG: OF 1876

The African Prince's
Drawing Room Entertainment . . .
Mr. Brown, having only just returned to this country from England,
will give a first-class European entertainment.

HANDBILL, CA. 1876

I am the Negro who'll coax a hoax.

I am a snarl who does know better, but . . .

I am the King of the Cool.

I am self-prized. I've had the South shown up.

I am all self-governed, bristled with the damn truth

I am a marquis who breaks yokes.

I am the remedy for your blind.

I am the lawful freeman. Part of you.

I am the enraged dancer, with a plan.

I am the black shout, man!

I am a will that's as powerful as my hue.

I have two eyes, shrewd and direct, both wise.

It is the Fourth of July.

The debt? One century's span

all spawned by the Designers, who'd forbid

me from grasping Thomas Jefferson's gifts

in vain, in vain, in vain . . .

I am Henry, a free black. My bliss is wry.

FROM DREAM SONG 22

FREEDSONG: DREAM SONG

Our Box Henry hid   away.
John Berryman's Ol' Henry sulked.
I see his point—he was trying to put one over.
It was that he thought that we thought
he *could* do it that breaks our Henry out this-a-way.
So, here he will come out and talk.

All the world like a fool-bent lover
once did see from Ol' Henry's side.
Here comes a departure:
hereafter, something falls out. Now, it might go fraught.
Let us see how Box Henry, pried
open for all to see, survives.

What he has now to say is a long
wonder the world can bear and see.
Once, with his black-face worn, John was glad
all at the top. And he sang.
Here, in this land where some strong be,
let Box Henry grow in every head.

FROM DREAM SONG 1

JUBILEE: GEORGE WHITE (1838–1895)

I stood still, like Ezekiel before wheels

of song one night when they didn't know

I was listening. At first, I couldn't quite feel

out what I was hearing. I heard them roll

betwixt sorrow and bliss in one note,

filling their throats with tears and spitting back

hope. They sing a strength I've burned to know.

So, while I lead this choir, I still find that

I'm being led . . . I'm a missionary

mending my faith in the midst of this flock . . .

I toil in their fields of praise. When folks see

these freedmen stand and sing, they hear their God

speak in tongues. These nine dark mouths sing shelter;

they echo a hymn's haven from slavery's weather.

JOHN WILLIAM "BLIND" BOONE,
COLUMBIA, MISSOURI: OCT. 25, 1925

*I interviewed Mr. Boone in the piano room of his spacious abode
in Columbia. Mr. Boone was well attired, and sat ever near to his ornate
Chickering Grand piano with which he punctuated our discussion.*

Thank you for your time, sir.

I wouldn't refuse a man who's come such a long way just to talk about ragtime. Besides, I can tell by the sound of your walk and the shake of your hand that you're carrying something heavy you need to put down. Or maybe you need help carrying it. And it's about music, eh?

Yes, sir. Scott Joplin in particular.

Scott Joplin. (*Sighs*) One of the best.

Before we begin: You sound a bit muffled. You intend to interview me with that cover on your face? Why you speaking through a mask?

It's a prosthetic, sir. A loss was suffered in battle.

I see . . .Well now, don't we make a pair. Two halves makin up a solid whole. I got no eyes, but all creation sees my face. You got vision, but most can't see past that mask. Folks know you, but they don't *know* you, and you're privy to a secret part of them just by how they act around you. And me, I somehow come to know every soul I meet. I can remember what they said ten years ago like it was yesterday, down to what we ate for dinner and desert. Everything except their face.

(*Laughs*) Don't worry. You the same as anyone to me, friend. I see past that mask of yours just like everyone else's.

Well, once again, thank you for your time, Mr. Boone.

And you going around asking folks all over, tryin to get Joplin's story, huh?

Yes, sir.

(*Laughs*) Well now. Looks like Scott got himself a straight man.

Excuse me?

An interpreter, son. An interlocutor. A straight man. Someone to guide us through the forest of tall tale and superstition. Sort out the foolish from the fact. That's what I smelled on you when you walked through that door. The scent of someone in search of a story.

Mr. Boone, I rather don't think of myself as a performer in a minstrel show.

Most don't. But fact is that the minstrel show is only a grin or a shuffle away from any living Negro trying to tell his own true, full story and survive in the world. The *true* story, now. There's a way to tell it straight and true, so that the joke's not on you, but all *around* you. The whole round riddle of it: how you came to be where you at, and what folks told you along the way that got you there.

Well then, sir. I trust that you may be able to help me get your own true thoughts on Mr. Joplin.

That I will, my man. The true story, 'cause I remember it all . . . *exactly*. Now, what is it that you would like to know?

For starters, Mr. Boone—how did you meet Mr. Joplin?

Ha! Yes . . . we met in the middle of a storm. He was scheming to take my money. But he was going to have to play that piano like I'd never heard if he was going to walk away with $1,000 cash.

Man walked in on a July 4th concert in Sedalia. '97. It had been thundering all that day, storming outside to the point where we almost called the concert off. Had to take it from the park to inside the old 400 Club, where all the colored swells would meet. If you wanted to get a nice crowd, that was the place to be. So, the rain was a bit of luck for me, 'cause it pushed them all inside to pay their money and listen to the music. I guess Joplin thought it'd be a little luck for him, too.

Like always, at the very end of the concert we issued our call.

Your call?

Challenge. Anyone getting up on that piano that could play something I couldn't play back, note for note, I'd give up a thousand dollars.

That's a lot of money.

It ain't nothing to sneeze at. But see, most folks don't want to risk getting beat by a blind man. Takes a special kind of person to duel it out with a man that ain't got no eyes. Some might say that kind of person ain't got no sympathy or class. And if they get beat, then folk might think they got no chops. And that's part of what we were banking on.

But then again, there was always those that thought I was a trickster or a con man, so they had to try. And then there were those who just wanted to match me. And those who wanted to learn. I couldn't tell which one of these Joplin was when he hollered out for the challenge and stepped on that stage. But I could smell the storm clouds on him when he walked up on there. Like he was draggin trouble at his feet.

And then it was what he said when he shook my hand—*Follow me.* (*Laughs*) All I could do was chuckle. And then he got on that piano. Commenced to playing a train wreck. (*Laughs*)

He was that bad?

Bad? No sir . . . wasn't bad at all. And he was damn full of himself, that's for sure. He got on that piano and announced, "Ladies and Gentlemen, a new composition of mine which you may purchase in your local store—a tune derived from the latest spectacle of Texas—*The Great Crush Collision March*!"

What a ham. I'm telling you, son—if I had any eyes, they'd've rolled all the way out my head just from hearing that. Had the nerve to saunter up on my stage and ring his own bell.

Yes, the Crush Collision March. *The one based on . . .*

A train wreck. That MK&T Railroad spectacle. '96. Those fools ran two locomotives together just to see what it would look like—and to make money from all the folks rollin in to see it. Had two old locomotives with boxcars full of steel face off, back up four miles apart, stuck the throttles in gear, jumped the crew off each one and let them roar at each other at 50 miles an hour each. Forty thousand folk showed up. Can you believe that? The things people pay to see. And people pity me while they're busy wastin their own sight. (*Laughs*) Them trains ran together alright. Both boilers busted, killed three people.

So this was when Joplin debuted that tune?

Indeed he did. Played it right there. His right hand was one train and the left was the other. Let me see . . . (*Plays*) Yes. That's it. Hear them two trains running at each other? (*Plays until the end*)

That's exactly how I played it back to him, too. Note for note, like he played it. But since he had to come up on my stage and bark a little, I was gone have to show him how to bite. I said, "Well friend, seems to me that if you want it to really sound like a crush, you ain't got enough crash in it yet. You got to lean on it a little to make that whistle blow." Something like that, is what I said.

So then I steamed it up a little, like so. (*Plays, accelerando while talking*) You hear them trains coming out that station? Hear them old engines talking, knowing they going to their final stop? Rollin full steam with no conductor for the first time! Whistlin down that track, all free . . . Hear that? (*Crescendo. Diminuendo*)

That's how to play it, friend.

Well, I could hear the crowd, but I couldn't hear much out of him. But he was standing there alright. Just heard a little cough. Then what I thought was a cough turned into a chuckle. And then I felt his hand on my shoulder. He leaned over in my ear . . ."Blind, huh? Not by a long shot."

"Very true, my friend, very true." We shook hands. He was still a ham, but I had to give him credit for walking away with dignity. Was a nice piece of work, that tune. Just needed a bit more drama in the execution. Worry about the wonder that draws folks in and the tragedy that strikes back when they least expect. You know, I heard tell that the photographer of that railroad monstrosity lost an eye from a flying bolt out of that train. Imagine that. Go to catch an image and end up losing an eyeball. Them was some spiteful trains, alright. I hope it was worth it . . .

So that was the last you met him?

Well, no. But I was rollin all over the place back then. Didn't stay home so much. I heard he'd moved to Sedalia. And of course, I heard all that ragtime he pulled out of his head. He'd gone and turned into a regular professor. Yes, I was hearing his name out in the world on a steady basis. And I heard that he'd found a bride and was starting a family. But Joplin, he was one of those people seemed like every step forward there was a step back. His baby caught consumption, died at six months. And soon after that, the marriage was done.

But his music? Just listen to it. (*Begins to play, phrasing songs as he goes*) Those tunes were just building up deeper and wider, like a plot of land where he was building a house, room after room getting added on . . . In one sunny parlor he'd have *The Entertainer*, in another room, with all the shades drawn, he'd have a *Something Doing*. (*Laughs*) And swinging on the porch, you got *Pleasant Moments* . . . Turn the corner and in the den there'd be *Swipesey* doing that cakewalk.

And then, he got himself a nice little garden all around the place (*Plays, referencing each rag*) . . . *Maple Leaf* . . . *Sunflower* . . . *Peach Tree* . . . *Pineapple* . . . *Weeping Willow* . . . *Chrysanthemum* . . . *Sycamore* . . . even a little *Sugar Cane*.

Yes, I guess you could say he was building a whole house of music—even when his own house was fallin down around him. I guess he was trying to build something for his next shot at life, you know.

So, when was the next time you met?

Well, I didn't really conversate with him much at all. Least not till he came back up on that stage with me again. That must've been around '05, I think. We talked twice. First time was at a concert in Columbia. I invited the maestro to come up and play a tune or two. And when he played them rags, son . . . let me tell you. Hot stuff. Seemed like I couldn't smell those rainclouds on him at all no more. He was full of sun, even when he had pain in his playing.

Turned out he was getting hitched again. Planning a honeymoon and all that. You should've heard him. Didn't need to brag much—his piano work did it all for him. But of course, he had to brag a little on his damsel. "I tell you, she's twelve years younger than me—but she seem like she been here before, you know? And man, I don't mean to . . . but if you could see her . . ."

"You forget, Joplin—I ain't blind. I hear her all over you."

And it was true. You could hear her in every note. You know, it was like he had her living up in that house with him. You could hear her inside them tunes when he played them, roaming around and sitting on the porch. Running 'round that garden, lying in the shade. You know, I never met her. But I know I heard her.

Anyway, like I said, Joplin was always one step up and then one back. And when they went on that train for the honeymoon and she caught cold, well . . . nobody could've known it would be pneumonia. And who would've known that she'd be gone after only two months?

Yes. I read about that. He was devastated with the loss.

Well, he disappeared for a while after that. Didn't nobody hear from him at all, from what they say. He was down. Down on the ground.

But then, when I was rolling through Sedalia on a concert a few months later, he came by after the show. 'Course, by then I had heard about his wife. But I could also hear something in the way he walked through the door, the way he said, "Hello, Boone," and just stayed all quiet. Something told me that her death was still ringing through him like a train of funeral songs that wouldn't stop. He was shook up—still a bit shaky on the edges.

I gave condolences and such, but he wasn't much interested in words. So, he sat at my piano. Just sat there for a while, not much to say. I could hear his mind working through what he was about to do. I could almost hear the music before he touched the keys. And then he asked me, "Can you follow this, Boone? I need to hear it from someone else. I need to hear it outside of me."

And so, that's when I heard her again. "Bethena," that's what he called it . . . One last dance. (*Plays while talking*) Took a cakewalk and swung it inside a waltz. Swaddled it up in rags and let it sing. (*Finishes playing*)

I've never seen folks dancing—but that was those two arm in arm right there. He got her living in that house of his, alright. Can hear them two-stepping plain as day.

So I sat down and played it back for him. Didn't change a note, though. Didn't change a phrase or a rest. It's like, if I could see—and I do see inside this song—looking inside their window, watching them dance. Can't change a beat. Don't speed it up or slow it down . . . don't want to mess with their time, you know. It'd be like tapping on the window when you're eavesdropping.

So, we just sat there awhile afterwards. I could hear him trembling just a little. He said thanks and joked about how one of these days he was going to win that thousand dollar prize of mine. (*Laughs*) That was the last I saw of him for a while. Didn't show up again until I was passing through New York.

And when was that?

Well, it was about a month before he went to the hospital, I guess. In '16. A few months before he died.

Knocked on my hotel room door right after a concert. I wasn't expecting him, so I guess he'd tracked me down. I was pretty easy to find, anyway. I patted him on the back as he entered the room, and I could feel how threadbare his jacket was—how skinny he had become.

I'd heard that he moved to New York with another bride and had set up shop trying to sell songs. But you know, people forget real quick about whatever joy you gave them if you ain't tickling them right all the time. And he had gone a nice spell without anything that made folks pay attention.

And then, you know, folks just don't listen to rags the way they used to. And here he was trying to make a ragtime opera. From what I heard, it hadn't exactly done well . . .

The score got critical acclaim, but the opera could never get enough financing. Not enough for it to be done the way he wanted. He debuted it once in 1915 in New Jersey, but he had no orchestra other than himself on piano, a small cast, a small venue, and a very small audience.

That figures. Folk ain't been lining up to see the old stuff for years now. Anyway, that night he was full to the top with the weight of worry. Could smell a blue hurt all over him. I could feel the tremor in his grip when he shook my hand. And that illness . . . like he was in its jaws and it was chewing him to the gristle.

Yes. By that time, the syphilis was pretty advanced. How was he able to play?

Well, he was able to do something. Something . . . different.

What was that?

He was trying to explain it to me, but it didn't make a lot of sense at the time. Was talking all in a jumble. Said he could show me the way. Said he had a storm inside his head and it was all from the future. Said he had a sky in his fingers that was all about the past. Was saying that over and over. And that he could show me the way. That only I could follow.

So, he was experiencing dementia?

That's what I was thinking when he sat down at the piano. He was still trembling when he got on that seat. I could almost feel it through the floor. He was telling me, "Follow me, Boone. Follow this." Mumbling underneath his breath.

And then he got real quiet, you know? Didn't hear nothing but his raggedy breathing. Sat there so long, I was thinking maybe he'd drifted off. And when he finally put his hands on the piano, it seemed like he was trying to rip it apart.

Now, I had heard stories that his playing had all but disappeared. That he couldn't make his fingers go the right way in the right time anymore. And when I first heard him banging all over that keyboard, I thought that the rumors must've been true. Sounded terrible, you know. And he was going on and on, with chords that didn't make sense, key changes that clashed, melody lines that got tangled up and thrown out with no rhyme or reason. Like that disease had gone and ransacked everything he'd learned—everything he'd built with his own hands.

But then, just as I was about to put my hand on his shoulder to stop him from making more racket, something started to sound different. I started to feel that music from a place that felt familiar, but distant. And I had to think and think and search myself to hear where it was. And it put me in mind of something that happened a long time ago.

You know, way back in '79 or so, there was a cyclone storm in Marshfield, Missouri. And this was a storm to end all storms. A whole pack of cyclones running wild. Lightning in their teeth and hell in their bellies. I mean, houses destroyed, hundreds of livestock slaughtered, and near 100 people killed along the way. Folks thrown through the air for miles till they landed with either broken necks, broken heads, or if it was a miracle, just a little bruising from a hayfield. Great Storm of 1879. You can look it up. Nearly wiped the town off the map.

I was about fifteen at the time. I was just in my first real chapters of how to make the piano truly speak like the world. I'd listened to that storm in the distance—it traveled close to 80 miles, so it got close enough to Columbia. I still remember the way that thunder sounded. Like God was tearing a hammer across the ground and stomping everything else in his path.

Anyway, that sound haunted me. It haunted me so much, I started to hear the music in it. And then later, I listened to the folks read the newspaper accounts. They felt like the world had been turned upside down and shaken out. And they all had something to say about that sound—like it was something they'd never forget.

So, as the weeks went by, I made a tune out of it, to remember how that terrible day sounded. I wanted to play it for the folk in Marshfield to let them know that their suffering was being remembered. Well, I finally had a concert down near Marshfield, and I got to play for them in a little veteran's hall—one of the few places left standing after the storm.

Well, at the end of the concert, I announced the tune, and I could hear it get a little more quiet in the room. I started up. It was going all good, I think they liked it—but then the rain in the song started to come up. By then, I was listening more to the piano than anything else, but I could sense a commotion going on in the room. I was busy trying to get that sound out of those keys—to bring it back into the room for just a minute . . . I wanted to show them that their pain was not forgotten.

Well, when I was finished, there wasn't no applause or nothing. The room felt different. Colder. Harder. My manager came up to me and whispered in my ear that about half the people had left the room and maybe I should leave the stage now 'cause they seemed pretty upset. That half the ones that were still there were crying silently or all huddled up in their chairs, rocking away.

I don't know how I missed that happening all around me. I usually hear everything. But then I figured out that I was in the middle of the storm, dead set in the eye of a hurricane, where everything got still, but the world was thrashing all around me trying to hold on.

And I didn't know what it must have felt like to be in that crowd till I heard Joplin playing that last time up in my hotel room. Somehow, he was making some kind of music out of that crazy mess he was finding in the keys. He was swinging somewhere between Liszt and spirituals, then lurching back into something gutbucket and backroom. It felt like he was inside that piano, fighting to get out from between the strings and hammers, and at the same time . . . hell, I don't know. He was fighting his way inside the music. Trying to say something older than all of us.

And it was something beautiful to hear. Awful, but gorgeous with its flaws. It was like that house he had built so careful over all those years had been picked up in a storm of his own making and destroyed—but then it was like all the pieces had landed someplace else upside down, folded into itself and then expanded into something bigger than itself at the same time.

And then it was done. And we just sat there.

How did you play it back for him?

Well, you know, I've had the same motto for 30 years. "Merit, not sympathy, wins." I started that because I didn't want folks to come and see me expecting to see a Blind Tom act. That man was a slave till the day he died. Barely knew it, too. When he played, it was like he was free . . . but . . .

I wanted them to know that I wasn't feeling sorry for myself—ain't asking nobody to come see me 'cause I can't see like normal folks—but to listen to me because you'll leave a better person afterwards. Enlightened, you know? From my darkness, you shall see light.

Understood, sir. I know a bit about that darkness.

But there's a flip side to that. I know what skills I got. You put anything down on that piano, I can play it back. And I ain't gonna have no sympathy for you no matter how broke down you are—'cause like you say, a thousand dollars is a lot of money.

More than a year's pay for most.

But, when I sat down at that piano for Joplin, it wasn't just my professional promise at stake. I wanted to play it back for him. I wanted to. I tried. I sat down and raised my fingers up to that keyboard, because I thought I knew exactly where to go.

But then, it's like a chill came over me. And I could feel that piano shifting underneath me. I'd never felt nothing like that. Never have since. But I could see that he had been playing a storm just like the same one back in Marshfield. I could see that we were like two leaves being blown all over the place in that storm, that cyclone that had thrown him all the way over to where he was, and that had set me down nice and easy into this house you're sitting in right here. I could see that, friend. Clear as day.

And I just couldn't get the nerve to roll up into that storm. I'd heard where it had taken Joplin. I'd felt it so close it made me want to be as twisted as that storm he had made—but I just couldn't bring myself to do what he'd asked me to do. So, I just sat there. I sat there with only the sounds of the birds outside and the wind and the trees. And after holding my hands over that keyboard for what seemed like forever, I felt his hand on my shoulder.

"Oh, yes . . . yes. I hear you, Boone. I hear you. Perfect. It sounds just like I thought it would. Thank you, friend." That's what he said. I swear before you today, he acted like he'd heard a revelation. He was smiling in his voice, and I couldn't tell if it was because he was mocking me, or whether he really thought he was hearing something.

And then he shuffled out the door. Left me sitting at that piano, caught up in the silence. Didn't call me on the thousand dollar wager or nothing.

And that was it?

That's the last I ever heard from him. I sent the money to his wife after my assistant tracked his address down. A bet is a bet. But I guess I don't mind saying that there's only one man won that bet from me. (*Laughs*) Finally lose that bet, and it's to somebody ain't even trying to beat me. Sometimes there's a good losing, though. Sometimes you lose at just the right time. (*Plays*)

JUBILEE: MAGGIE PORTER (1853–1942)

This choir helps me brave the hard weather

when I sing lead soprano. Even when

the concerts are relentless, we remember

ways to keep our faith alive. We get pent

up in sweltered railcars and cold hotels with

drafts—but the hymns roar on, nevertheless.

They blast through our throats, beating injustice

and those who'd see us bent to ignorance—

like when the Ku Klux burnt down the schoolhouse

where I taught one Christmas. They couldn't stand

to see us rise up from plantation dust. How

they must have angered to see me teach again . . .

We won't stop our music until we're through

tearing down Jericho's walls with our truth.

C

my motto for life

    —merit, not sympathy, wins—

        my song against death.

ROOTS OF BOONE

My roots burrow down
to Col. Daniel Boone
and his frontier town
of Boonesborough, where
the brown-skinned dwellers
were his, bought and paid
for by the folk hero
of wild liberty, the bowie-
knifed fighter of Indians.
They were my kin, those
slaving in the shadows
of history. Transports
from African shores
to Ol' Kentucky,
and later Missouri.
I've often wondered:
when Boone was taken
captive by the Shawnee,
when they kidnapped
members of his family
and he was forced
to scramble for his life,
if he stopped to ponder
on the lives he'd bonded
into slavery . . . perhaps he did.
I'll never know if he ever
once intended to free

the slaves of Boonesborough . . .
he never made it so.
Seems one man's master
is a country's idol
when one side of the tale
is all that gets shown.
Well, either way,
those kin survived long
enough to get me here
on this piano—where
I can sing on these keys
the notes they might've
sung if Daniel Boone
had truly lived
his legend of freedom.

$E\flat$

i stroke piano's

eighty-eight mouths. each one sings

hot colors of joy

BLIND BOONE'S BLESSINGS

John William "Blind" Boone caught encephalitis at six months.
The treatment was removal of the eyes.

Bless the fever in that night
in the sixth month of my life.
Bless the fever, for it gave me sight;
it swole my brain to fit God's gift.
It brought the hand that would lift
each eye from my infant skull.
Bless the sweat; my baby bawl.
Bless the horse that hauled
the surgeon through dusk's dark,
half drunk and swearing, into mine.
Bless the flame—it sterilized
the metal of the spoon. Bless
the path between lid and bone,
slipped and slid by that instrument
of my deliverance from sight. Bless
the handling of the knife. Bless
that night that gave me night,
wrapped it 'round my bloody
face, whispered how I could be
grace notes, arpeggios, a piano roll
of sound copying each note
from everything around me.
You see, I'm sure at first
there was the hurt

and the scalding pain.
But then again, bless
an infant's too short
memory. All I know is
what lies beyond light.
I've learned this is what's right
for this one right here. Yes, bless
the fever, then listen close.
Spare an ear to this piano
and shut your eyes closed . . .

F

pentatonic black

keys raise up high into bliss,

born to sing my name

BLIND BOONE'S VISION

When I got old enough
I asked my mother,
to her surprise,
to tell me what she did
with my eyes. She balked
and stalled, sounding
unsure for the first time
I could remember.
It was the tender way
she held my face
and kissed where tears
should have rolled
that told me I'd asked
of her the almost impossible—
to recount my blinding
tale, to tell what became
of the rest of me.
She took me by the hand
and led me to a small
sapling that stood not
much taller than me.
I could smell the green
marrow of its promise
reaching free of the soil
like a song from Earth's
royal, dirty mouth.
Then Mother told me

how she, newly freed,
had prayed like a slave
through the night when
the surgeon took my eyes
to save my fevered life,
then got off her knees
come morning to take
the severed parts of me
for burial—right there
beneath that small tree.
They fed the roots,
climbed through its leaves
to soak in sunlight . . .
and so, she told me,
I *can* see.

When the wind rustles
up and cools me down,
when the earth shakes
with footsteps and when
the sound of birdcalls
stirs forests like the black
and white bustling
'neath my fingertips,
I am of the light and shade
of my tree. Now,
ask me how tall
that tree of mine
has grown to be
after all this time—
it touches a place
between heaven and here.
And I shudder when I hear

the earth's wind
in my bones
through the bones
of that boxed-up
swarm of wood,
bird and bee:
I let it loose . . .
and beyond
me.

F ♯

whippoorwill, hawk, crow

sing madrigals for blind men.

Forest blooms through each note.

BLIND BOONE'S ESCAPE

Even a blind man might run away
from folks that won't see things his way—
That's what I told myself when
I packed my bag and bailed out
of the St. Louis School for the Blind.
My whole town had pitched in
for tuition, dime by dime, 'cause
we'd been told they'd teach me
more piano. They did, for a time—
and I'd fallen hard in love with
its ivory lessons. But then? Listen—
the new schoolmaster came to say
that piano was to stay clear of black
hands and our unlearned ways.
I was banned from the music room
and given straw to manufacture
brooms with my other colored mates.
But who was this fool to decide
my fate? I fumbled my way out
the school's back gate. I'd been swept
out by their broom philosophy,
straight into the streets of sweet
St. Louis. Her alleys and gangways
awaited my touch. I struck out
toward the salt sticky sounds
of barrelhouse drama. Toward the
pimps and johns and cathouse

groan that seemed to run on
syncopated piano and moan.
I could smell the sin and taste
the grown-up rum of laughter
spilling under a setting sun . . .

Damn, I was dumb. Could've
been killed. But still, here I am.
And I will remember that night
under a sky that I knew must be
stuffed with a million tunes
I could almost hear from my
grassy bed. I'll never forget . . .
I leaned in to wear it like a bowler
tipped hard across my head.

G

my eyes: buried deep

    beneath earth's skin. my vision

begins in her womb.

BLIND BOONE'S RAGE

Can a blind man kill and walk away?
Can he find the jugular and slide
a blade through the dark, through
the vein—and then escape?

That's what I'd ask myself
in the thick of those days
after I'd run away from home to make
my mark with a would-be manager.
I'd trod his roads for weeks—
but instead of money, he'd speak
of sudden fees I owed. How my debts
had grown and signed my folks into debt—
that they'd find themselves sued
into ruin if I didn't grind those piano keys
like his trained monkey. This went on
night after night, while in the day
I'd be confined to locked rooms.
Nobody'd listen to a ten-year-old's
plea for freedom. He'd tell them
I was in his charge—and a little slow . . .
and soon enough I began to know
my mother's slavery—note by note,
song by song. He took the one thing
I truly owned and smothered it
with hate till every finger I lifted
for music bore the weight of shackles

and chains. And so, I started to wonder . . .
about making a blade. How to break
a glass clumsily and smuggle secretly
one long, slick shard. How to wait
for the dead of night to cut him hard
and dead. Yes, my friend. I'm sorry
to say that I felt this the only way
I was going to win myself back again.
I'd gotten low enough to start planning
the spill and the strike—to prepare
myself perhaps for prison . . .
so it was a damn lucky thing when
my stepfather finally tracked me down
in the midst of my labor, claimed me
for kin in his iron clench and hauled me
over his heaving shoulder, stomping
through the saloon's battered door.

I swear it now and I swore it then—
I'll never slave my music for no man
again. I ain't bendin over no piano
like a plow on a sharecropper's piece.
I ain't no beast bent to push ivory keys.
I'll be free as I play or I won't play at all
—I'll just play the notes inside my skull
alone in the dark where they roam
around loose. 'Cause playing like a slave,
I'd just step myself straight into
a hangman's noose.

B♭

darkness sounds like God

   flowering from earth's molten tomb . . .

writhed wind. chorded cries.

BLIND BOONE'S PIANOLA BLUES

They said I wasn't smooth enough
to beat their sharp machine.
That my style was obsolete,
that old rags had lost their gleam
and lunge. That all I had
left was a sucker punch
that couldn't touch
their invisible piano man
with his windup gut-
less guts of paper rolls.
And so, I went and told them
that before the night was through
I'd prove what the son of an ex-
slave could do: I dared them
to put on their most twisty
tune. To play it double-time
while I listened from another
room past the traffic sounds
of the avenue below.
To play it only once,
then to let me show
note for note how that scroll
made its roll through Chopin
or Bach or Beethoven's best.
And if I failed to match my fingers
and ears with the spinning gears

of their invisible pneumatic piano
scholar, I'd pay them the price
of a thousand dollars.

And what was in it for Boone?
you might ask . . .

Might be the same thing that drives men
through mountains at heart-attack pace.
Might be just to prove some tasks
ain't meant to be neatly played
out on paper and into air,
but rather should tear
out from lung, heart, and brain
with a flair of flicked wrists
and sly smile above the 88s . . .
and, of course, that ever-human
weight of pride that swallows us
when a thing's done just right . . .
But they were eager to prove me wrong.
They chose their fastest machine
with their trickiest song and stuck it
in a room far down the hall from me.
They didn't know how sharp
I can see with these ears of mine—
I caught every note even though
they played it in triple time.
And when I played it back to them
even faster, I could feel the violent
stares . . . heard one mutter,
   Lucky black bastard . . .
and that was my cue to rise,

to take a bow in their smoldering
silence and say *Not luck,*
my friend, but the science
of touch and sweat and
stubborn old toil. I'd bet
these ten fingers against any coil
of wire and parchment and pump.
And I left them there to ponder
the wonders of blindness
as I walked out the door
into the heat of the sun.

ʊ

rain, flower, sea, wind

    map my dark horizon. i

        inhale earth's songbook.

JUBILEE: GREENE EVANS (1848–1914)

Tearing down Jericho's walls. Spreading the true

mission of Jubilee—to wage righteous

battle 'gainst slavery's law-scorched falsehood

that one man may own another. We're just

giving witness when we sing, the same way

Joshua blew his horn—which must've sounded

to them fool Rebs like Yanks charging straight

on. My brother and I got blood-hounded

hard when we escaped ol' master. By then,

we too had heard Union bugles blow. We knew

it was the fall for Jericho. My friend,

can you imagine how it must feel to

finally own your own skin? Arms? Legs? Eyes?

To bellow with your own almighty light?

CARMEN LEDIEUX, 544 WEST 123RD STREET, HARLEM, NY: JAN. 26, 1926

Where were you when you first heard Mr. Joplin?

I was a boarder in his house on 47th. But let me ask you this: How did you find me?

Well, I got your name through a Mr. Sam Patterson. He said he knew you as a resident of the Joplin house.

Piano Sam Patterson?

Yes . . . a piano player. A friend of Mr. Joplin.

Sam Patterson . . . Damn, now that's been a dog's age since I seen Sam. (*Laughs*) Glad to see he still remembers.

He had good things to say.

Yes, I bet he did.

So . . . let me ask: Did you hear much of Mr. Joplin's playing?

Why you want to know?

Well Miss LeDieux, I'm just interested in the stories he left behind.

Look. Ain't no niggers rollin all over the country just lookin for stories 'less there some money attached to it. What kind of stories you lookin for? And what you got to give for these stories?

Ma'am, look. I'm just a coal thrower trying to find out a story. I don't have a lot to give back other than your own recollection. Only thing I can really promise you is that I'll pass it on.

So you going across country, lookin for stories for free?

Yes ma'am. I travel.

I see. And what's in it for you?

The stories, ma'am. The stories. I want to send them out to get published. So the world can know who . . . how he was.

And what they pay you for these stories?

Not much, if anything. Maybe enough to pay expenses. There's a satisfaction in that.

I see. And where you from again?

Cairo, Illinois.

Cairo, huh? I'm from just up the Muddy in Paducah. They was lynchin a whole lot of niggers in Cairo. You lucky you left outta there before you was lynched yourself.

My cousin was one of those lynched. That's why I left.

I see. Well, I can't make up my mind if you smart for leaving Cairo, or dumb for roamin around lookin for a dead man's story. 'Cause I ain't never met a nigger so stupid as to search all over for the story of a ragtime man ain't nobody heard from in years. Why you choose an old piano man like Joplin? I mean, he was good, but wasn't no Fats Waller. Now *that* nigger can *play*. Wasn't no Willie Smith, neither. Damn sure wasn't no James Johnson.

He came before all of them, ma'am!

So what? That don't mean he worth ridin all over the country to tell his story. Ain't no nigger on the planet I'd be traipsing that much for. What's so special about his story you need to be botherin folks about the past?

Well, you have to know the past in order to understand the present . . .

Yeah, but let me tell you: ain't nothin *to* understand when you hear the present in the music. You just know it for what it is, and your foot gets to tappin and everything else flow. You take this jazz music . . .

Exactly, ma'am. They took his music and . . . tricked it out until it was way too . . . too steamed up. That's why I . . .

What you say? "Steamed up"?

Boiled all up like a boiler ready to burst. See, I . . .

That's crazy, son. I'm telling you, maybe you lost a little more than you care to say beneath that mask and all—but that ain't make no sense at all.

I saw it ma'am. I saw it being changed when I was overseas and the James Europe band played all across France.

James Reese Europe. Now *that* was a man folks want to read about. Why ain't you write on him? I know lots of folks want to read about the leader of the Clef Club. Worst day in Harlem when his drummer cut his throat.

No, ma'am. I mean, yes, it was tragic and all. But I think folks want to read about you and what you know about Joplin. They want to hear your piece of his story. It's an important story, much more important than those other musicians'—he taught them where to go with the music they make, the music they've changed into their own. He was there first. He was a teach—

First? What you mean first? I'm starting to think maybe you should've stayed in Cairo. Look, if Joplin was before them other piano playin niggers, you can bet your life there was a whole long line of other niggers before him. And if they wasn't playing piano they was on a drum or a dance or something. He told me that himself once. Said it in the middle of one of his tantrums. Said he was lookin past the past and syncopatin into the future. Quiet man, but sometimes he riled up when he got stuck.

He said that? See, that's the kind of thing that folks want to know. The small things—anything you can remember . . . So please. Tell me more.

That's the kind of story you want?

Whatever you've got. Please.

Well . . . seeing how as you ain't lynched yet . . . guess you need these stories more than I do. Maybe there's a little I can recall.

Let's see. When I got a room with them it was just uptown from Tin Pan Alley. He and his wife had music. I had guests.

I see. You were a . . . hostess?

Hostess? If you want to call it that. I wasn't robbin nobody or cheatin nobody and what my guests paid for they got with pride. In the end, I paid my rent on time. The Joplins were good with me, long as there weren't any ruckus up in my quarters. I was independent. Always have been. A lot of the women there was what you call "hostesses." We made do, and made do for a lot of family down South, whether they knew where the money came from or not. That's how I bought this here boarding house.

Did you hear much of his music there?

Are you kiddin? How could you not hear that piano clinkin all through the day and night? Wasn't nothin but chords and choruses runnin all through that neighborhood anyway—but his sounds, they seemed a lot more older than the rest. Seemed a little more restless, but all ancient at the same time.

How do you mean "ancient"?

I mean passed down. You know—parable old. You know how you hear somethin new, but after you hear it, seems like you couldn't have done without it, like it was waitin there to be heard all the time and how could it have been missed before now? That was him. Played every chord so much we boarders couldn't help but know damn near every note. I guess you could say we were his first audience in New York. We heard every movement get spawned and shucked. Many times we'd hear that piano rise and roll from daylight till midnight. That building was soaked with his sound. Breathin his story all over us.

Did he talk much about his music?

Well, that time I told you about before was about the time when I moved in. He wasn't much into talkin.
There was another time though, if I recall, when he seemed a bit under the weather. That was later on, when he stayed mostly to himself and Lottie. I asked him about one of those tunes, one he had been working hard for weeks.

What did he say?

Well, I asked him what that type of music was. That it seemed like he was tellin a story that hurt to be told. I tell you, he looked at me like I was about to soil his sheets of music, then he just walked away. I figured anythin hurt that much wasn't worth draggin out.

Do you remember the music he was playing or how he practiced?

There was this one part he was playin—it felt like a branch of pine with a rough notch in it that wasn't quite gettin smoothed down. He was trancin it over and over and over, spellin up the whole building.

It was gettin to be like some kind of wall opening up between anyone in that building and the world outside. A wall that had doors with missin knobs. Had knotholes and splinters and screens where there should've been windows—and everything you could peek at on the other side was rusted with hope—you know, the kind of hope you know ain't gonna come back. That's a kinda hope you gotta have when you got mouths to feed that you ain't even seen in years. You gotta give up a part of you every hour to get those morsels, and that music was . . . (*Hums a bar*) . . . still remember it now.

You mean, Treemonisha?

Is that what he called it?

Yes, ma'am. An opera. He performed it back in '15, in Jersey.

Opera? Didn't sound like no opera to me. That's just like him, though. Niggers makin operas . . . Sounds like somethin he would take up. He get rich off that one?

Well . . .

Of course not. You know why? He was a nigger. Makin operas. Ain't nobody gone see no niggers makin no operas. Even niggers ain't gone see no niggers playin no nigger operas. Bless his heart. With all that playin, he shoulda stuck to Tin Pan Alley. He still had it, most times, when his blood didn't slow him down too much. Floundered on that keyboard from the fresh-broke light of damn near every early morning except Sundays. All them stammered up chords and barrel rolls and two-steps. He changed them out each morning like dirty linen. He'd keep at it, too, till late night, till that piano box shut with a fist bang. Then it was all his murmurs and curses roamin up and down the staircases. Was all caught up in that opera story, I guess.

Did you find out what the story was about?

Was it about a woman?

Yes.

Mmm hmmm. Of course it was. Of course . . .
    Well now, look. I believe I've spent more than enough time talking about the dead with you today. I'd best be about some live folks' business. Take care now, you poor fool. You keep on looking for your ol' raggedy-time stories. Bless your heart.

JUBILEE: ELLA SHEPPARD (1851–1914)

She got filled with the Almighty Light—

that's what stilled Mama's hand that summer night.

I was only four. She grabbed me by her side

and dragged me to the river, set to die.

I'd fallen for my mistress's candy bribe,

snitched on how Mama had "borrowed" rice

from the big house. Good Lord, the cost of that.

Till then, I'd never seen my mother slapped.

She shook. Smoldered. Then dragged me to the river

to drown her daughter who had learned slavery

so well, along with herself. *I'll never*

let them twist you so! she said. That very

moment came a voice from ashore. Aunt Ruth

shouted: *Stop! Have faith! We can pray this through!*

BERT WILLIAMS/
GEORGE WALKER
PARADOX

THE WITMARK AMATEUR MINSTREL GUIDE

and

BURNT CORK ENCYCLOPEDIA

REVISED AND COPYRIGHTED MCMV BY M. WITMARK AND SONS

A minstrel entertainment gives the young amateur rare opportunities to display talent in the vocal, comedy, and dancing lines. No form of entertainment is so replete with comedy, nor gives such universal satisfaction when well represented. It affords vocalists a chance to *come out* in solo or concerted work, and the young comedians or dancers excellent opportunities to *shine forth* and give full vent to their humor and wit. Minstrelsy is the one American form of amusement purely our own, and it has lived and thrived even though the plantation darkey, who first gave it a character, has departed. The dandy negro has supplanted him but the laughable blunders are still incorporated by the negro of the present time. The ballads of Stephen C. Foster breathing of slave life and the cotton fields, have been laid aside for the modern love song with a dramatic story or descriptive ballad,—yet the minstrels sing them and the change from ante-bellum days from the darkey to the present time, has been accomplished without perception. Minstrelsy is the most popular form of entertainment and is always selected as a vehicle to present the talent of the club, college, school, or association. With this in view, the present book is compiled and arranged to instruct, suggest, and prepare minstrel entertainment perfect in all its details— from the "blacking up" of the artists to the fall of the curtain upon the concluding burlesque. Everything has been arranged in the most simple manner to assist the aspirants in their preliminary efforts, *detail* being the watchword. The ladies have not been forgotten, for be it recorded that it is quite the fad for ladies to "black up" and give a minstrel show.

* * *

IMPORTANT INSTRUCTIONS

In rehearsing the gags with the end men, be careful to impress to them the necessity of selecting those of a varied nature in order to avoid similarity of subjects. One end man may represent the enlightened, sarcastic darkey; another, the dense fellow—jolly, but ignorant. Still another, the imitative or declamatory darkey, whose *forte* seems to be poetry or recitations; then again, you can have a sleepy, blundering fellow, mispronouncing words and totally at sea concerning etiquette or history, there being enough material in this book to suit all.

* * *

HOW TO BLACK UP

AN INSTRUCTIVE OVERVIEW

First we get a lot of champagne corks, or remnants of cork from a cork stopper factory. These are placed in an old tin pail—which serves as a furnace—and then ignited. A few holes in the pail, which furnish draught for the blazing corks. When they have been thoroughly burned, they are crushed and reduced to powder by hand. Then this powder is moistened with water, and we run it through a small paint mill to grind it fine. Then we place the paint just made into tin boxes and it is ready for use. You moisten with a little water the quantity you need as you are applying it to the face.

* * *

It has been the aim of the writer to provide for the young amateur a gold mine in which to delve and draw forth "chunks" of fun, to spring upon his audience, and he has also endeavored to make this book a veritable encyclopedia of everything pertaining to minstrels; at the same time he has not forgotten to build a work to which the reader can turn and peruse, when seeking funny literature, or a remedy for that tired feeling called *ennui* or the blues.

ALL COONS LOOK ALIKE TO ME!

A Chant of Merry Coon Song Melodies

GUARANTEED! *ALL TITLES HISTORICALLY ACCURATE!* **GUARANTEED!**

1

["All Coons Look Alike to Me"] caused a lot of trouble in and out of show business, but it was also good for show business because at the time money was short in all walks of life.

ERNEST HOGAN

A Coon Band Contest

A Coon of Pedigree

A Coon Possum Hunt

A Coon Wedding in Southern Georgia

A Night in Coontown

A Royal Coon

All Coons Look Alike to Me

Bedelia, The Irish Coon Song Serenade

Captain of De Coontown Guard

Coffee Colored Coon

Coon Blood Is Bound to Show

Coon, Coon, Coon

Coon Hollow Capers

Coon Jine

Coon Jine, Baby, Coon Jine

Coon Jine My Lover

Coon Schottische

Coon, That's Noise to Me

Coon Town's Vacation

Coon With the Big Thick Lips

Coon, You've Done Me Wrong

Coonology

Coon's Birthday

Coon's Paradise

Coon's Salvation Army

Coonville Grand Cakewalk

Da Swellest Ladies' Coon

Dar's a New Coon Wedding

I have often sat in theatres and listened to beautiful ragtime melodies set to almost vulgar words as a song, and I have wondered why some composers will continue to make the public hate ragtime melodies because the melodies are set to such bad words.

SCOTT JOPLIN

COON SONGS MUST GO!/COON SONGS GO ON (1)

A show goes	all 'cross country,
to a	farmland
country town	or big city—
—some low down	uppity Negroes put
loudmouth	blame on a
coon shouter	minstrel for how he
sings	moanin'
"Coon, Coon, Coon"	
or some other song	—but we wear blackface
that has plenty of coon in it	to make white folks' truths easier,
with an emphasis on the word coon.	to mask the ugly in their mirrors.

Left side is excerpted from "Coon Songs Must Go!" *Indianapolis Freeman*, January 2, 1909.

2

With the publication of ["All Coons Look Alike to Me"], a new musical rhythm was given to the people. Its popularity grew and it sold like wildfire.

ERNEST HOGAN

De Coon and de Chicken

De Coon Dat Had de Razor

De Coon from North Carolina

Happy Hours in Coon Town

That Coon Town Rag

That Strange Coon

The Cockney Coon

The Coon from the Moon

The Coon That Stole Ma Honey

The Coon with the Big White Spot

The Coons Are All A-Dreamin'

The Coons Are on Parade

The Coons on a Lark

The Coon's Trademark

The Coontown Regiment

The Counterfeiter Coon

The Dandy Coon's Parade

The Hottest Coon in Dixie

The Laughing Coon

The Laughing Little Red Head Coon

The Mormon Coon

The Oriental Coon

The Phrenologist Coon

The Real Coon Dancing

The Shuffling Coon

The Stuttering Coon

The Wedding of the Chinee and the Coon

There's No Coon That's One Half So Warm

I have often heard people say after they had heard a ragtime song, "I like the music, but I don't like the words." And most people who say they do not like ragtime have reference to the words and not the music.

SCOTT JOPLIN

COON SONGS MUST GO!/COON SONGS GO ON (2)

In this way	I make cash—
and in many other ways	I give white folks giggles
too numerous to mention	when I wear blackface. Yeah, them
"coon" songs	
have done more	earnin' much bread. Want
to insult the	highfalutin'
Negro and cause	hilarity with
his white brethren,	laughing all 'round? Crackers,
especially the young generation,	they want to see unrefined niggers:
to have a bad opinion of	the way they think we are. There ain't
good Negroes and bad Negroes,	but one kind of coon they want. And more . . .
than anything that has ever happened . . .	they want it made true for them on stage.

Left side is excerpted from "Coon Songs Must Go!" *Indianapolis Freeman*, January 2, 1909.

3

["All Coons Look Alike to Me"] opened the way
for a lot of colored and white songwriters.
Finding the rhythm so great, they stuck to it . . .
ERNEST HOGAN

Every Race Has a Flag but the Coon

I Wonder What Is That Coon's Game?

If the Man in the Moon Were a Coon

I'm a Lucky Coon

I'm a Mean Coon When You Rile Me

I'm the Father of a Little Black Coon

I'm the Toughest, Toughest Coon

Little Alabama Coon

Little Coon Lullaby

Ma Rainbow Coon

Mammy's Little Pumpkin Colored Coon

Money Was Made for Coons to Spend

Mr. Coon, You're All Right in Your Place

My Little 'Lasses Candy Coon

Mysterious Coon

New Coon in Town

No Coon Can Come Too Black for Me

No Coons Allowed

Oh Mr. Coon

Oh Susie! (Dis Coon Has Got de Blues)

Oh! You Coon

Old Zip Coon

Only a Little Yaller Coon

Red Hot Coon

Sue, Sue, What's a Coon to Do

Susie-Ue Coon Song

Traveling Coon

When a Coon Sits in the Presidential Chair

Whistling Coon

You'll Never Find a Coon Like Me

If some one were to put vulgar words to a strain of one of Beethoven's beautiful Symphonies, people would begin saying: "I don't like Beethoven's Symphonies." So it is the unwholesome words and not the ragtime melodies that many people hate.

SCOTT JOPLIN

COON SONGS MUST GO!/COON SONGS GO ON (3)

The colored man writes the 'coon' song,
the colored singer sings the 'coon' song,
the colored race is compelled to
stand for the belittling and ignomy of
the 'coon' song,
but the money from the 'coon' song
flows with ceaseless activity
into the white man's pockets . . .

This song that I sing. Do you know how
twisting beauty into ugly burns?
Believe this: ain't no way I'd take a
insult if I weren't getting paid. Yes, I sing
—it keeps a belly full. That work
just enough to feed my own. I sing
to put clothes on my baby's back.

Text on the left is excerpted from the *Indianapolis Freeman*, August 24, 1901.

DUNBAR-BOOKER DOUBLE SHOVEL

Paul Laurence Dunbar Meets Booker Taliaferro Washington

We wear the mask that grins and lies,
It hides our cheeks and shades our eyes—
This debt we pay to human guile;
With torn and bleeding hearts we smile . . .

PAUL LAURENCE DUNBAR, "We Wear the Mask"

TABLE 2-3

BLACK VICTIMS OF LYNCHINGS PER 100,000 BLACKS BY STATE, 1882–1930

STATE	NO. PER 100,000
Mississippi	52.8
Georgia	41.8
Louisiana	43.7
Alabama	32.4
S. Carolina	18.8
Florida	79.8
Tennessee	38.4
Arkansas	42.6
Kentucky	45.7
N. Carolina	11.0

TABLE 2-5

THE REASONS GIVEN FOR BLACK LYNCHINGS

- Acting suspiciously
- Gambling
- Quarreling
- Adultery
- Grave robbing
- Race hatred; Race troubles
- Aiding murderer
- Improper with white woman
- Rape
- Arguing with white man

- Kidnapping
- Terrorism
- Courting white woman
- Killing livestock
- Testifying against white man
- Criminal assault
- Living with white woman
- Throwing stones
- Cutting levee
- Looting

- Incest
- Rape-murders
- Arson Inciting to riot
- Resisting mob
- Assassination
- Inciting trouble
- Robbery
- Attempted murder
- Indolence
- Running a bordello
- Banditry
- Inflammatory language
- Sedition
- Being disreputable
- Informing
- Slander
- Being obnoxious
- Injuring livestock
- Spreading disease
- Boasting about riot
- Insulting white man
- Stealing
- Burglary
- Insulting white woman
- Suing white man
- Child abuse
- Insurrection
- Swindling
- Conjuring

- Train wrecking
- Defending rapist
- Making threats
- Trying to colonize blacks
- Demanding respect
- Miscegenation
- Trying to vote
- Disorderly conduct
- Mistaken identity
- Unpopularity
- Eloping with white woman
- Molestation
- Unruly remarks
- Entered white woman's room
- Murder
- Using obscene language
- Enticement
- Non-sexual assault
- Vagrancy
- Extortion
- Peeping Tom
- Violated quarantine
- Fraud
- Pillage
- Voodooism
- Plotting to kill
- Voting for wrong party
- Frightening white woman
- Poisoning well

JUBILEE: THOMAS RUTLING (1854?–1915)

I thought I'd lost faith. Couldn't pray my way through

the last time that I saw my mother

in life. I still feel the burnin' lashes they threw—

here—on my arm, where they whipped to make her

let go. She went crying down the road. Dragged . . . slow.

Chained to a wagon pulling her off. I

still remember how she sang that Bible, though.

Sweet Chariot. Roll, Jordan Roll. I try

sometimes to hear her voice in mine. The choir

helps with that, I guess. I can just about

feel her holding me still, like when we'd hide

in the woods, away from master's blight. How

long did she live, I wonder? And did she die

dreaming of our flight, hands clasped, into starlight?

LOTTIE JOPLIN, PART 1,
NEW YORK, NY: MARCH 11, 1926

This interview with the Widow Joplin transpired during the fading days of winter in the brightly lit and spacious living room she once shared with Mr. Joplin on 131st Street.

Mrs. Joplin, thank you again for spending your time with me.

Well, folk come through all the time here paying respects. Wish they was paying a little more than respects, but I do fine. I been blessed.

Well, thanks again for your time. I wish I...

Now, you say you work on the trains?

Yes ma'am. Engineering.

Engineering?

Yes ma'am. Engineering an iron shovel into a bed of coal. Used to be a Pullman before the war, but... these days I cause less commotion when I'm shoveling coal rather than serving drinks.

I see. You must be good at what you do if they let a Negro anywhere near the engine.

I do my best ma'am. You know they don't like workin with us.

And in your off time you look up musicians, eh? You want to know about Mr. Scott Joplin?

Yes, ma'am.

Well, if you want to understand how Scott lived, you got to know what was taken from Scott. What and who he lost. All that got stolen away. You got to know who Treemonisha was.

Treemonisha? Treemonisha was his ragtime opera. You must have seen him compose every page of it. What was his inspiration? I have quite a few...

Slow down now, son. See, Treemonisha was not just an opera. Treemonisha was his family. She was all he had left, besides me. She was almost all ghost. And more than a little bit of haint. But even more than that . . . She was *alive*.

Now, don't you look at me all squinched up like that. I know what I've seen. And more than most, I know what I've heard. See, I lived with her for seven years. I saw her grow, note by note, under my roof. Between me and Scott. Holding us apart sometimes, bringing us together mostly. I could hear her running wild up and down the staircase of my house. I could just about see her sitting on Scott's lap at the piano, teaching his hands where to go on those keys.

You're trying to tell me that Treemonisha . . . was a spirit?

Look, boy. What good music you know ain't got a spirit to it? Ha! Write that down!

Mrs. Joplin . . .

Rest easy, son. I got reasons for telling you this. See, Scott told me a few things a lot of folks don't know. Now, you may know that Scott was married before me.

Twice.

Yes. Well, his second wife, Freddie . . . when she died only ten weeks after they'd been wed, he felt quite a bit whittled down. Like he couldn't get his brightness back, I guess. When I met him, he was just past the midnight of his mourning. Bless his raggedy soul.

And so, one night, after we'd got to know each other good enough, he told me some things he didn't like talking about much. He wouldn't shake it loose until I pulled it out of him—else he would've carried it with him to the grave. See, fact is . . . Freddie was carrying a little tune of her own, a whole 'nother composition inside her . . . she was growing his child.

They'd found out soon after she went ill, after the doctor examined her and all. They thought for sure she'd get over that pneumonia. Had their hearts set on a girl. And she wanted that child to be named Monisha.

Like the girl in his opera?

That's right. And the first time I saw her was the first time I saw Scott in concert.

You actually saw her?

That's what I said, ain't it? Let me back up for a minute. Now, I'd met Scott because he wanted to rent a room in my building. This was when I was living near 27th Street. He needed a big room that could hold that piano of his. My building not far from Tin Pan Alley was just right for him at the time. He moved in, and right off you could tell that something different was happening when he played that piano. See, I've had more than one piano man as a boarder. But when that one played, it seemed like some kind of light was rolling through the building. Seemed like things just started to slow down, too—but not in a bad way. Just in a way that made the sun sit in the sky just a little longer than usual, and the moonlight to fall a little thicker after midnight.

That sounds a bit superstitious, ma'am.

That sounds like it should've been my first clue, that's what it sounds like. But I didn't have any way of knowing at all until I saw her up close.

I see. How close were you?

Like I'm seeing you right now.

Mrs. Joplin, I don't think . . .

You the one wanted to know about the King of Ragtime. You writin this down? You either writin or leavin. Which one it's going to be?

I see . . . Yes ma'am. Please continue.

Now, I went to see him play one night not long after he'd moved in. Went down to the Diamond Stud on Second Avenue to see him play. I'd *heard* him play in his own room for weeks, but never *seen* him play at all. He was so shy and quiet all the time, just going straight to his room and setting down to push those keys around. I wanted to see what was causing all that strange flood of light waving through my building. I wanted to *see* up close what was running in his heartwork to make his hands syncopate so hard.

Well, he got up on stage and played all his old rags, the good-time stuff. Showed us how a rag's supposed to fit all nice over your body like a new set of tailor-made Sunday bests. How it's supposed to patch up all the holes you got from wanderlusting too far and too hard. He was a professor in a church of lost souls. We were all in the pews of his fingertips.

But then, he dead-stopped in the middle of one of those rags. Just plain quit. His brow wrinkled up, like he was readjusting himself inside, feeling for a rhythm he'd lost. Then he looked down, and put his hands in his lap. I swear, he looked like a prayer had just fallen over inside him.

He closed the lid on that piano, and we thought it was over. Folks were quiet, for a minute. But then someone from the back started to yelling about "Where the damn music at?"

He snapped out of it a little bit then—but only came out of his trance long enough to pick up the lid on that piano again, and put his hands down ever so slow on the keys. Then he pulled a long, heavy waltz out that piano—the kind that'll make ivory speak in tongues—that'll make wood call out its natural tree name.

Do you know which rag it was?

Shush. I'm in the middle of telling you right now. You stay writin.

Now . . . he was more slow and careful with this one, not like those other rags. This one he was rocking gentle back and forth on the bench, but swayin that piano sound across the room so hard till it rained an ocean we were all wading in. By the time he had finished swaying that piano all over us, by the time he had rocked that piano back to sleep and let it be just plain old wood and wire and bone again, seemed like all the air had gone out the room. (*Laughs, slightly*)

Came to realize it was really just me holdin my breath all that time.

But for just that reason, I thought maybe I had been hallucinating—seeing visions from the belly of that tune: a glow holding tight to Scott on his little bench, swaying back and forth with him. It was that same kind of light I'd seen in my building when he practiced all day in his room. But when he was playing, I could see it just as plain as I see you. And I could tell he was listening to it, talking back to it on that piano.

When that piano stopped ringing, it took everyone a little while to get hold of themselves. Well, by the time folks had decided to start clapping, he'd turned away from that piano and left the stage.

I didn't see Scott again until midnight. Seems he'd gone straight home and gotten right on that piano in his room. Played up until twelve, and would've played longer if I'd let him. Had to knock on his door to let him know that I got other boarders paying good money to sleep at night—and to thank him for the concert just as much. When he opened his door just a peek, I couldn't help but also ask him the name of that last piece he played, even though he was acting like he just wanted me to go away. He spilled it out, real quick.

"Treemonisha." He said it with his breath all hushed up, his eyes looking down at the floor. And somehow, right then, I knew. I knew enough to ask, at the least.

And so I did. I said, "That's some right proper mourning, Mr. Joplin. She's still with you, you know that?"

Well, we talked a long time that night. Seemed like he had needed someone to lay down his story to. Someone to understand along with him about what was happening in his music. We talked for a long while. He started humming the tunes in his head real soft so as not to wake up the tenants, and next thing you know, he'd held a whole concert just under his breath, telling a vision that had Monisha as alive in his voice as if she'd been sitting right there with us.

So, Treemonisha *was the rag he played that night.*

I keep telling you, boy. She wasn't just a rag . . .

Yes ma'am. She was alive.

Write it down, now. You write that *down.*

JUBILEE: JENNIE JACKSON (1852–1910)

Mama and us fled, hands clasped, into the light

of a Nashville dawn, running from rogue slavers.

Our presidential last name wasn't quite

enough to outshine this skin. Was never

worth much till Andrew Jackson passed on. Left

my Granddaddy George free. Then there was me,

Mama, and her washboard legacy. So she bet

my future on some university

schooling. Had no idea I'd be singin'

slave-cabin-kindled songs all 'round the world.

I've been educated on European

soil, between concerts. I bet I've traveled

more than ol' Andrew on this rambling mission

to prove how our souls are holy and human.

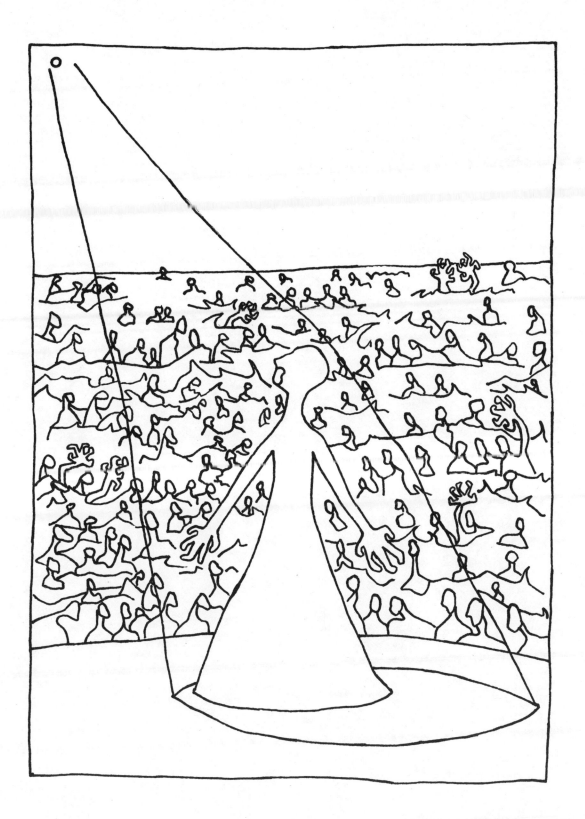

Works Progress Administration Field Interview

Text of Interview (unedited)

Name of worker: Eva Shoe

State: Ohio

Address: 1229 West 5th Street, Dayton

Date: March 12, 1935

Subject: Medicine Shows: Minstrel Shows.

I run my own show now. But back in the day I used to work for Black Patti. I got on with her troupe 'cause I know how to twist myself into knots until most people can't tell where I begin or end. Folks used to throw pennies for applause and I'd have the floor shining in copper. Don't bend quite 'xactly like that no more. But back in the day, like I said, folks used to line up for blocks to see all of us. The mighty Black Patti Revue. Each one of the crowd wantin to see her belt it out the way the white folks would do—even better. All that pearly white song flowin out that pretty black skin, all that European sound spillin out that Ethiopian river of a throat. There was quite a few fellows wanted to proposition her, dreaming about how they'd wake up to hear history in their bed every morning, a history they wanted to own past the skin they lived in. But she wasn't much feelin any kind of special from them. She was mostly caught up in the truth she was workin out of each note. She wanted to resurrect all the church she could muster out of those opera stories. She wanted to muscle arias out all those spirituals.

MY NAME IS SISSIERETTA JONES

Once word got out about the way I sing, the world wanted to bleed all the sass out my name. To scratch out the gift my mother gave me and shove a would-be white diva in my spotlight. They couldn't imagine the colored in *coloratura* standing on its own onstage, so they claimed I was just part of Adelina Patti's chorus. They stuck me beneath her name, a shadow sentenced to the borders of her light, called me Black Patti.

But the darkened sense inside my name won't be silenced. With its *sister* and *shush* and gospel of ocean, I sing each night from the way I'd stand on the docks of Providence, a straggle-boned bundle of lungs and tremble lifting wave after wave into wave after wave of Atlantic. Its applause keeled over me, calling me with its bell of salt, its belly of sunken hulls, its blue green fathoms of tremolo. Every night, in the dark offstage, I hear my mother's voice in my head, her backyard hum, the sea in her distance with the weather of storm. She'd look out and see the thrall of water heave its back to the sky. I'd look out to the darkness and hear my true name.

Thing is, you wrestle too long with someone else's song, you gotta make sure you find as many ways as possible to make it your own. But you still gotta remember where the line is between you and that other song, or you gone get your voice all grunted up—confused. That's what she was wrestlin with. Sissie—or Miss Jones to anyone who ain't know her good—that's what she'd tell me. I know she didn't think I was listening most of the time, but even then, when I was just a small time sand dancer and contortionist, I would hear her talking about how she would make herself one with those arias and then snap back into spirituals like daytime turning into night and back into day. Like a two-headed doctor of song. She was oceanside born, you know. Right off the Atlantic. Seemed like her voice had a tide in it that tied all time together. She'd turn all your moments inside out. Seemed like sometimes she'd take a whole year's worth of seasons and pour it into one moan, standin up there with her mouth swallowing up everyone's sorrow one note at a time.

SISSIERETTA JONES, CARNEGIE HALL, 1902

O patria mia

Aida, buried in the darkness
of her fate. Aida, singing
in the tomb of her lover.
Her lover a notion pale as
the aria circling from her mouth.
Aida, lowered into the pit
cloaked in breath's ocean,
a war inside her voice.
A battle of tongues sung *doloroso*,
the husk of shadow on air.
With the soar of her father's
sermon for truth. With the burn
of nigger heaven. With the hum
of oceans wrapped in bone.
With the legacy of bones
wrapped in ocean. With a national
healing hogtied to song.
Let me hum it to you sweet
with *vivace*; let me scrape it into
our history. Let my voice turn
its scarred back on you.
Let my skin disappear
to cover you whole.
Let my molten song be
your blessing of ash.

Let the ash cover all
our faces. Let ash be
the secret that masters
itself. Let the curtain rise
upon the hidden face.
Let the spotlight burn
to purify need. Nail down
the lockbox of spirituals
inside my throat. Bury
them in opera's echo
of grandeur. Resurrect the holy
grind of *tremolo* and tradition.
Let the key be infinite.
Let the coon song scatter.
Let each mouth be envy.
Let bloodlines be muddied.
I stand solo in this country
of concert. I am multitudes
of broken chains. I am Aida
with war on her lips.
I am Aida against drowning
in all that summons her alive.
I bear the crescendo
of ocean inside me.
I carry its bones inside
my attack. I am a wave
reaching beyond this shore.
Let this belting be our
unbinding. Let *o* bring
the sound of all our wanting.
Let *patria* speak the names
of all my fathers.
Let the curtain rise

to show the face that is
known. Let the country
be mine. Let the country
be mine. Let this country
be mine.

Of course, even when she did belt out some opera born outside of this country's peculiar history, she'd still have to come right back down and weave her way out of the cakewalk of blackface and jim crow. Every evening, she'd waltz all proper out of the spotlight—and then let the okie doke shuffle and that coontalk grin take over the stage. You know—the circus they was all comin to see. All of 'em—black and white and every shade in between—came because of her name, wantin to see the famous Black Patti herself. And just about as many stayed on to feel the glow of those minstrel shines. What is a coon show, anyway, but one poor devil puttin on a mask another devil willin to pay to see?

SISSIERETTA JONES

ad libitum

I sing this body *ad libitum*, Europe scraped raw between my teeth until, *presto*, *Ave Maria* floats to the surface from a Tituba tributary of *Swanee*. Until I'm a *legato* darkling whole note, my voice shimmering up from the Atlantic's hold; until I'm a coda of sail song whipped in salted wind; until my chorus swells like a lynched tongue; until the nocturnes boiling beneath the roof of my mouth extinguish each burning cross. I sing this life in testimony to *tempo rubato*, to time stolen body by body by body by body from one passage to another; I sing tremolo to the opus of loss. I sing this story *staccato* and *stretto*, a fugue of blackface and blued-up arias. I sing with one hand smoldering in the steely canon, the other *lento,* slow, languorous: lingered in the fields of *Babylon's Falling* . . .

ut through another. She'd even raise a toast to the mask
d that the opera was wearing her as a mask, or if it just
Was it her voice or someone else's? they'd seem to ask.
or in just plain old American, went straight down to her
She'd pour those opera songs all over her body and then
ne time, that in order to hear her true voice, she'd had to
ht I have on? she said. *Because let me tell you, most don't
which masks, how many masks you're wearing before you
ey know just how to slide in and out of it, how to make the
song all over that mask and make it one with the world, no*

SISSIERETTA JONES &
THE BLACK PATTI TROUBADOURS

Forte/Grazioso

Forte—with force was the will that overtook me, that freed my throat and lit my mouth to music. *Forte* was each wave of song, *forte* like my father's choir of freedmen, sometimes wavered and off key, sometimes pitched in more fear than light, but always *forte*, hurling what voice was left to them into the cauldron of church air after lifetimes singing their spirituals in secret. They sang *forte* like the stevedores' shout from ship to shore, crate after crate of cargo burdened into the holds, their gandy opera bouncing off hulls, *forte* in the *grazioso* of their motion, the all-together swing of arm and hand and rope and hoisted weight, *grazioso* onto decks all braced for storm, all blessed with prayer from each Providence pulpit, prayed over from bow to stern, blessings from the communion cry of each church, all *grazioso* with hands raised in testimony. I hear them each night, *forte* when I stand on our prow of stage from town to town, port to port, captain of this ragtag ship of blackfaced, cakewalking fools and balladeers, teaching crowds *grazioso* under spotlights with each ticket sold. *Forte* is the cry of the barker bundling each crowd with the smooth-talk promise: darkie entertainment with a touch of high-class classical. *Forte* is the finale each night, *grazioso* is the closing curtain, the unmasking of painted faces, the darkened lamplight, the applause fading like the hush of receding surf that carries us on through the night, the ocean of audience rising and falling with each wave of season, *grazioso* is the sail of our bodies in their wind.

That's what I learned from the great Sissieretta Jones. How to know where the mask begins and you end. How to balance the world on edge just between that mask and you, until the mask melts away into mirage. Took what she taught me and then I moved on. I'd saved up all those pennies from the crowds to buy me a proper little horse and wagon and a proper little medicine-show stage to haul around the country. You know, I named it after a sign—what my plantation-born daddy and his daddy was chasin and what we all still after. That North Star. We the North Star Travelin Negro Troubadours. You should come on and see us when we roll through your town.

JUBILEE INDIGO

(CHORAL)

How do we prove our souls to be wholly human

when the world don't believe we have a soul?

How do we prove black souls holy and human

when the whole world swears we got no souls?

We hitch our voice to heaven's sword-tongued plow

and sow the seeds of a righteous mission.

After we've spent our voices up, how we know

these old cabin songs make a difference?

After we've run our lungs ragged, how we know

these hand-me-down hymns make a difference?

We'll know by the hushed wonder that follows

our song. We'll know by the heated silence.

We'll sow this heavy sack of achin

hymns, seedin' sable soul 'cross every nation.

LOTTIE JOPLIN, PART 2,
NEW YORK, NY: MARCH 12, 1926

*An impromptu visitor for Mrs. Joplin had interrupted our previous
interview session. We renewed our interview the next evening.*

Mrs. Joplin, I was wondering if you could explain something to me.

I can try.

Treemonisha, the character in Scott Joplin's opera, was an advocate of education. She was clearly opposed to superstition and the ways of hoodoo. She rallies her town against a local witch doctor and leads the fight against conjuration and superstition.

Yes. That's true.

So how is it that Mr. Joplin was claiming that he was haunted? It seems to me he was far too rational a man to buy into these notions of haunts and haints and whatnot. Isn't that a huge contradiction?

Superstition ain't real. Treemonisha *was* real. Real as you. But not to all the senses all the time. Seems like I could *see* her when he couldn't see her, but he could *hear* her all day, plain as day. That is the manner by which Mr. Joplin—and, I guess, myself—was haunted.

Well, if he was so . . . haunted . . . that you got haunted too, how did you bear it?

Let me tell you this: I've known a lot of men in my life, to one extent or another, and almost all of them haunted. Some haunted by their past, some by what they see in their future. Some haunted by what could have been, others haunted by what never was and what they never had. Other men haunted by lies, and others by too much truth. But they all haunted by the same thing. Fear.

So many of them carry that tombstone of fear on them some way or another. They try to run away or run around or climb over and under that fear, but they got it hanging all over them like weight deader than a graveyard.

Scott Joplin? He was not the least bit scared. Not a twitch. He held his haunting next to him like it was another heart in his chest. He wasn't afraid of losing his family, 'cause they'd already been taken. Wasn't afraid of loving them, 'cause that's all he had left for them. They worked a power on him. And they wanted to be heard. To speak out loud and sing and stomp their feet. To be alive again, at least in the air where folks could hear them. And that's what Scott was bound determined to do. That's how he grew Treemonisha up and put her in the world, no matter who tried to steal her away from him.

She'd tell him secrets. She'd tell him the past and the future. The way it was, the many ways it might have been, and the way it was going to be. And then she'd tell the way she wanted to be heard in the world. She'd tell him this all at once when he was working all that ivory, kneading it back to life and making it speak.

That spirit even told him that his body was breaking down, how there wasn't much left of his playing days, how his days on the planet were numbered. How his blood had gone way too bad way too quick, and that he had a bit less than a decade left.

He knew all this, and still he had no fear. He knew his pain, now. He could see the tremors and the feel the chancres and the taste the grief in his future . . . But he'd still not buckle down into fear.

You write that down, son. Write it down for forever. You write, "He was not afraid of his fear."

"He was not afraid of his fear." Yes, ma'am . . .

See, most men afraid to be afraid. They got fear, most of all, *of* fear. And that is what this spirit, this Treemonisha, taught him to tame. To tame it like a woman.

Like a woman? To tame it like he'd tame a woman?

Now you trying to say what I ain't said. Listen, and write this down: to tame fear like a woman tames fear.

A woman knows fear from the beginning—that what she has to look forward to is fear. We're told to fear the pain of birthing, and we keep on making the world come out of us. Told to fear a man's hand when he's angry, and we keep on saying truth that turn men into fists. Told to fear being a woman, 'cause it means we only get half the credit for twice the job—and we go ahead and hunch it up anyway. Told to fear loving a man 'cause it'll break us in two, and then we go ahead and love a man so hard it's enough for a dozen. We're told we can't get what a man has, and we go on ahead and squeeze it out the world's grip.

We're told a woman hasn't the smarts to own a building, like the building you in now that's got my name on the title. We're told we'll have to get a man for a scrap of loving and a piece of roof, and when we get all that without them we're told we'll be lonely forever after. We're told that if we use what we're born with, and what may be the only piece of ourselves we got left that men will pay cash for to make our living, then we're evil and lost, and we'll starve out the rest of our days all loveless, low, and broken. And then we take that fear and heal ourselves whole.

This is the fear I'd been told from birth. And I testify that fear is a devil's liar. This building? I paid for this building—me and me alone. Hustled up the down payment by crook and by hook. Rented to all kinds of folk to raise the scratch that paid this building off. Musicians working overtime, gamblers working under the table, women under my roof negotiating for themselves what a pimp in the tenderloin would want to take for free and retail top dollar. As long as they got that rent up, we were all good.

Fear. I got no use for it. Fear never paid one bill nor put one morsel in my mouth. You can write that down.

Yes ma'am. It is written.

Now, like I said, Mr. Joplin didn't have no fear. But he might as well have had a fear of accounting. I'll tell you—he was the King of Ragtime, but fact is he was damn near the Duke of Debt. I mean the man had no real head for business—not really. I helped him rearrange his finances so he could make a decent wage off his music. And that's partly how I know for sure about how that Berlin stole from Treemonisha.

How is that?

Berlin. You know he can't read music too well, right?

Irving Berlin? But he's a prolific composer . . .

That does not mean he writes music, son. It means he hears it and gets it written. And that's exactly what happened with him and Treemonisha. See, Mr. Joplin and Berlin shared a studio at their publishing company. I was with Mr. Joplin on the day that he played out the last parts of Treemonisha in that very studio.

Thing is, Berlin later on said that if he could find a man who could make a hit like the one he made, he'd pay him a bunch of money and then choke the rest of his songs out of him. Well, he didn't have to choke a single soul to fetch that tune out of my husband, and he has not rendered a single dime to his estate. But he owes him that much and more. Much more.

I can see him now, playing that piano with Treemonisha's glow all over him, laughing and cooing all in his ear while Berlin stood over in the corner, mesmerized. You know, I think Berlin might've seen that Treemonisha himself. Took her home in his head and swapped her clothes up. Changed her name and fixed some face paint on her. Steamed out her stride and called her Alexander . . . I know you've heard Alexander, now.

Alexander?

Real popular. Had his own band. "Alexander's Ragtime Band," he called it.

You're saying that Irving Berlin stole "Alexander's Ragtime Band" from Scott Joplin?

I'm saying what I saw and what I heard. I saw Scott playing the "Real Slow Drag"—that's what he called Treemonisha's finale—right in front of Berlin only months before he came out with that song. I'm saying I heard that same tune running through the streets and ringing out of pianos all over New York, and I saw Scott's fists clench up when he first heard it.

I can remember what he said, too. Said she'd been kidnapped. Said he felt like he could hear Treemonisha "ramblin drunk all through Tin Pan Alley." How she'd been "smeared with burnt cork."

I remember him going home and playing all burnt up with loss on his piano for days after he heard that Alexander tune. He was conjuring up Treemonisha, trying to riddle out a way to reclaim her.

That's what he did, too. He took her step and poured some more song in it. He took her swing and swung it out a bit further. He turned her dress from calico to silk and wrote her a new smile with a little more grit.

So he rewrote her finale?

Exactly.

Well, why didn't he sue? Berlin earned a mountain of money off of that tune.

Well, he was going to. But, he reasoned it out with Treemonisha and changed his mind. She told him to let it be—that he ain't have time to chase after the shadow of the creation they'd sung together. She told him he only had a few years left, and that if he spent time chasing after what was stolen off him, he'd never be able to see her dance tall in the world. If he went chasing in the courts for white folks' justice, all he'd see was a hard and lost time, and that he might as well just change her dance ever so slightly and sharper and move on. So that's what they did.

Still, Berlin owes the estate thousands and thousands of dollars! Those are your royalties now, are they not, Mrs. Joplin?

True. I believe so.

How will you ever regain all that money if you don't go after it in court?

I think I explained that to you, son. Ain't you been writing none of this down? Or maybe you just ain't listening too hard. Scott made a peace with that trouble before he died, and his work told him to let it go.

And it got replaced with a farce. It seems to me that this is part of the problem with us, ma'am. That we don't make it our business to get paid fully what we are owed. Who will we have to blame when what we have is stolen if we don't at least try to wrestle it back?

You really ain't been listening too hard have you, boy? That man spent all his life wrestling with the music and that piano and his troubles and his ghosts . . .

And he wrestled it all that time just to let it go? To let Berlin walk away with the last of his work?

To let go of something he was never going to get back no way. Don't tell me you ain't never lost something ain't worth trying to get back. I know you must know about that, seeing how you wear your suffering all over your face.

Mrs. Joplin . . .

I'm sorry for that. I truly am.

But just like you ain't gettin your face back, Scott wasn't going to get that part of his song back. Ain't nobody going to get nothing back from the past except stories you can wear to put your life straight. You've got to know that if you know nothing at all.

Now, I know the value of inheritance and money and all it means to the world. Leastwise, I've got enough of it that I'm standing in right now to let me know how hard it is to let go even the tiniest piece of it. But I watched a dying man come to terms with what was left of his past . . . and learn to love any pain of the present. And I learned, in the hardest way, in the worst way, how to love it too. I learned to love it, and to walk away when it was done with me. And I am done with it.

Let them have Alexander. I know where he came from. I know who his daddy was and how he came into the world. He got kidnapped away once, but he's making out alright while he's passin on Broadway I guess. Got his face and his name changed, but I know he still one of us. He knows it, too. That's something no court of law can take away or give. Take one listen at him and you can hear Treemonisha smirking right underneath his breath. He's been stolen off, but that ain't nothing new for Negroes—and he's doing a whole lot better than most other song spirits I've known.

I got other things to look after rather than chase the ghost of something stole from me I ain't gonna get back. I've seen enough of that by now. You might want to consider that. You might want to take heed.

Still, all that money Berlin made off that tune.

Yes. That's true. And it's a lot more than that as well. But in the end, it ain't nothing I'm gone miss more than Scott. Ain't nothin more than that.

Look, I'm not going to deny that you're right. I tell you what. You tell Mr. Berlin, if you run into him, that I accept checks if he ever wants to pay his due to Treemonisha. You do that, and I'll just be waiting here for that piece of mail . . . till the day I die. (*Laughs*) Now, you *definitely* write that one down.

BERLIN V. JOPLIN
ALEXANDER'S REAL SLOW DRAG

Two years or so ago,   I heard my kidnapped tune

when "Alexander's Ragtime Band" was a big hit,   ramblin drunk all through Tin Pan Alley. Then, I heard

someone started the report   'bout the minstrel leer it wore

among the publishers   smeared with burnt cork. I know

that I had paid   ragtime's cost—Its

a   bright

negro   treasure . . .

ten dollars   ain't no price

for it   I'd take . . . .

and then

. . . I'd just

published it under my own name.   had the chance to name it: "Real Slow Drag."

When they told me about it,   I 'spected Berlin was the thief—

I asked them to tell me   —and was right: I knew whom

from whom   to blame.

I had bought my other successes—   Straight from my gut, I'd made other hits,

twenty-five or thirty of them.   but this one was my dusky gem.

And I wanted to know,

Why can't some folk handle

if a negro could write   tunes as good as my own

"Alexander,"   —and not steal?   *Me?*

why couldn't I?   I refuse to thieve.

Then I told them | That thief schemes 'bout
if they could produce the negro | music. He wanted Black gold . . .
and he had another hit | snatched from me. He craved dark sounds,
like "Alexander" in his system, | his soul corked charcoal, his skin staid white.
I would choke it out of him | If I could—I'd stain him brown,
and give him | naps on top,
twenty thousand dollars | royalties damned to hell
in the bargain.

. . . then I'd ask him

If the other fellow deserves the credit,
why doesn't he just go get it?

Left side: Irving Berlin's reply to rumors regarding theft of Scott Joplin's "Real Slow Drag" from the ragtime opera *Treemonisha*, published in *Green Book Magazine*, April 1916. Right side: Joplin's imagined response.

174

IMMANUEL CHRISTIAN FELLOWSHIP, PORTLAND, OR, 1996: GREATER JEFFERSON BAPTIST CHURCH,

EATONTON, GA, 2000: STUBBS CHAPEL BAPTIST CHURCH, MACON, GA, 2000: NEW EVERGREEN

BAPTIST CHURCH, MACON, GA, 2000: BETHLEHEM AME CHURCH, MACON, GA, 2000:

JUBILEE MISSION

(CHORAL)

We'll haul these hymns 'cross every destination

that's never heard The Word wrung through dark

skin. It's our mission to birth a brown, human

voice bustin' into freedom. Up from scarred

and brambled paths we've stumbled 'long from one

generation to the next—without rest,

with soothin' found only in what we've bled from

the flesh—ourselves and our song. And yet . . .

we've mostly owned our songs more than ourselves.

So, we've chose to sing up heaven rather

than dwell down on plantation's minstreled

shuck and buck. Our home is our voice, gathered

and honed and whetted and sharpened—

cuttin' slave days down to sermon up salvation.

ST. PHILLIPS BAPTIST CHURCH, SWAINSBORO, GA, 2000: ALL FAITH FAMILY WORSHIP

CENTER, AMERICUS, GA, 2000: ROBERSON GROVE BAPTIST CHURCH, WAYNESBORO, GA, 2000: MT.

HOPE AME CHURCH, MACON, GA, 2001: HOLLY SPRINGS BAPTIST CHURCH, WASHINGTON CO., GA, 2007:

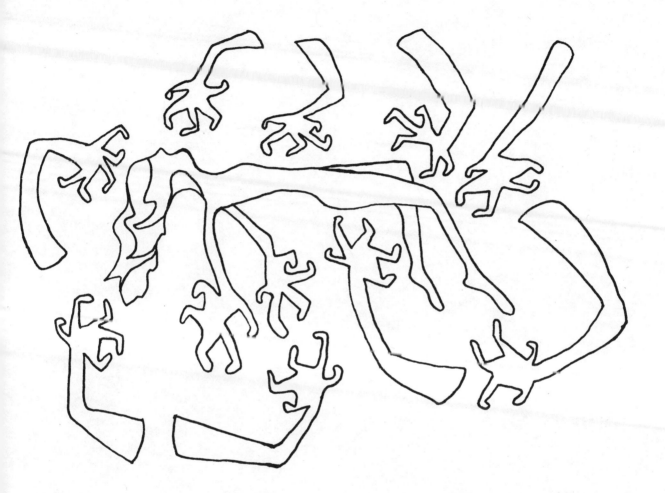

I was . . . declared to be wild—they could do

nothing with me. Often they said to me, "Here is

your book, the book of Nature; come and study it."

ALABASTER HANDS

Edmonia Lewis, 1862

Let me tell you how
white hands kilned me
in the moonless middle
of night. How they stripped
and spittled and smeared me
in an open field hardened
with ice. How they worked so
diligently upon me with palm
and fist and angry sweat,
with knuckle and dirty nail,
until I was struck still as stone,
until I was one with the dust
of the Earth that called my name,
whispered to me from its labyrinth
of lava and buried bone. My truth
was honed there, deep in the fated
crease between life and loss.
It willed me to rise from the dirt
and staggered me home.
I claimed for my own
what they'd strived to strike
from me. I scraped myself
up from what they'd tried
to beat down. And now
I let them witness how

artfully their curses fold;

how ruthlessly I mastered

their death-less hands

beneath the weight

of my mercy-fraught mold.

1872. Wildfire sits at her workbench in a small studio in Greece, the summer trees pulling shade into her studio. Before her, a mound of alabaster heaps beneath her hands. It swirls like an unsung song beneath her palms. She listens with her fingertips to the bones buried in the clay, the flesh and vein and tendon waiting to spring from dirt. One decade earlier, she lay beneath Ohio stars like a fallen comet, she lay beneath fist and footstomp, she waited between life and death like a bare-skinned burn in the winter snow and stared at the stars tilting above her. She waited for the hand of mercy.

FOREVER FREE

Edmonia Lewis, Marble, 1867

What a thing it is
to be delivered
from beneath
the dirt,
from hardship's
rubble,
from underneath
the feet
of the world.
To raise up
on one's own
pedestal
and become
bondage's living
tombstone.

1862. Wildfire lay not far from the campus of Oberlin, where her older brother had sent her to learn how to mold herself into a brown survival of whiteness, her brother who had moved out west and made money from the gold rush had come back to rescue his little sister, he had come back to his homeplace in New York to retrieve his sister from her Wildfire ways in the midst of her people, where she sold weavings and carvings with her mother, listening to the ways of her languages through her mother's tongue, to the tourists. Oberlin, her brother had heard, was a place of refuge, a place of learning where the whites were human enough to see past the color of her earthen skin, where she would be molded into something beyond her mother's Ojibwe and her father's runaway blood of Maroon, where the language and the writing and the music would seep into her bones and grow her a new tongue, where she would learn America from the front steps instead of the back door, where her intelligence could be chiseled into a finely pointed tool.

HAGAR IN THE WILDERNESS

Edmonia Lewis, Marble, 1875

My God is the living God,
God of the impertinent exile.
An outcast who carved me
into an outcast carved
by sheer and stony will
to wander the desert
in search of deliverance
the way a mother hunts
for her wayward child.
God of each eye fixed to heaven,
God of the fallen water jug,
of all the hope a vessel holds
before spilling to barren sand.
God of flesh hewn from earth
and hammered beneath a will
immaculate with the power
to bear life from the lifeless
like a well in a wasteland.
I'm made in the image of a God
that knows flight but stays me
rock still to tell a story ancient
as slavery, old as the first time
hands clasped together for mercy
and parted to find only their own
salty blessing of sweat.

I have been touched by my God
in my creation, I've known her caress
of anointing callus across my face.
I know the lyric of her pulse
across these lips . . . and yes,
I've kissed the fingertips
of my dark and mortal God.
She has shown me the truth
behind each chiseled blow
that's carved me into this life,
the weight any woman might bear
to stretch her mouth toward her
one true God, her own
beaten, marble song.

Wildfire meets the young white women of Oberlin, the chalk- and petal-skinned women of progress, the ones that would invite her over for dinner, who agreed she was surprisingly bright, diligent, clever; who had never had a conversation with a person so dark that had lasted longer than the air necessary to give a command, they were breaking bread with this small tornado of black/brown bloodline, this amalgamation of savage literacy who seems to absorb books like she is drinking from a freshly found stream, this walking, talking wilderness inside the walls of Oberlin, wandering around and soaking up the light of the Humanities, of the Great Civilizations, this woman come from a potion of wanderment and wantonness. They invite her into their libraries and lecture halls, they burnish their tongues to her on the struggle between civilization and anarchy, between womanliness and wildish ways, on blue and gray Fort Sumter cannon and Bull Run grapeshot, in a time of blood upon blood upon blood.

HIAWATHA

Edmonia Lewis, Marble, 1868

I spawned deep in Earth's muddy womb
when man's folly was mere rumor.
But a colder, more chisel-wracked
drama came when sculpted rock
made me human figure. I'm myth,
conjured from Ojibwe legend,
doctored into Longfellow's pen;
Wildfire palms bore me into form.
My stare hammers across all time—
it heaves through mountainous empires,
haunting gunpowder's religion
of blossomed bone and blood that pumps
the pilgrim's locomotive heart.
My creator made me noble
witness to her art of would-be
witness. Her hands delivered me
through history, hauling her own
soul—you can see it written here
in these eyes she carved into stone.

They would let Wildfire entertain them, on some nights they would gather at her room and listen to her tales of living off the land, of reveling in the rhythms and songs from the earth where all known creatures were buried, and one night they gathered and toasted, they all drank gladly, and when two of Wildfire's friends went out later for a romantic sleigh ride with two young men who might later be Union officers, who were courting their fevered embrace, the women fell feverishly ill while on their rendezvous, were discovered to be nearly mortally ill, were hospitalized. They told authorities that they must have been slipped a faulty aphrodisiac by Wildfire, that she must have wanted them to be unduly enticed by their male company, that she was responsible for an elixir had clearly delivered them nearly to death. And as Wildfire denied poisoning the young women, denied dosing them with a deadly potion that would serve her no earthly purpose, the young suitors on the sleigh ride went unmolested, unsuspected, and unaccused, and one night

THE DEATH OF CLEOPATRA

Edmonia Lewis, Marble, 1876

She reached into the ground
with saw and sluice, chiseled
me down from mountainous
till I was almost mortal, perched
me in the throne of Life's last
promise. She fashioned me
a legend unlocked from Earth's
history. Her brown hands
bore me alabaster smooth
from rubble to royalty,
birthed mo into the breach
of my last breath, baptized
me in the burn of her sweat
over my every ripple and curve
to teach me love like the blows
of a million small hammers
in search of the stillborn heart.
And while she polished my demise
with pumice and her slow, grinding
work song of muscle and scrape,
I learned the labor of a queen
robbed of country, of a Creator
who carves her story into the face
of all she beholds and bids it shine
until Death's garden of stone
is ground to Life.

Wildfire is surrounded by those that would avenge the alabaster women. She is encircled by an army of palms, there is burlap over her face, there is abduction to an empty field, words and accusations and vows that blossom into one slap, then another, a torn cloak, a knee into spine, a fist into cheekbone, a clamored clawing for safety, a blood spray across snow, a shredded skirt, a scalp pulled bloody by the hair, a plea for mercy, a pillaged flag of blouse, a whitish hand upraised against the night and swiftly falling again and again into and against her vision, a nakedness she had never known, the snap of civilization bearing its mark across her bones, a breath expelled beneath a broken rib, the literal booted foot against the back, there is a sinking into earth, there is surrender in a brown, beaten theater of war, and then, finally, blessed abandonment. The silence of the North Star beaming in its distance.

INDIAN COMBAT

Edmonia Lewis, Marble, 1868

We three warriors
were called forth
to be, forever, enemies.
Stolen from marble,
pressed into slaughter,
we never weary. We
seek no asylum except
the perpetual hatchet,
the eternal blade,
the never-ending arrow,
our fists that swallow
our senses till we've carved
ourselves into memorials
for causes long forgotten.
Our fight was forged
by a free brown woman's
brunt, her design for
all our fates entwined
like fingers laced in prayer
for victory, then mercy,
then dug into the Earth
to resurrect our embattled
lives lived just as her own:
pounded into memory
with mettle on stone.

Wildfire lay near extinguished beneath the heavens, lay there until discovered by searchers, lay near the end of one story and the beginning of another, lay listening to the voices she heard when she was so close to the earth's embrace, listening and listening and listening more than she had ever known possible to listen. She is beginning to know that she knows the language of the earth. By the time she hobbles into a courtroom to be tried for charges that two young suitors never had to answer to, by the time she has mended enough to attend the trial that might put her away for life, she is hearing the voice of the earth inside her bones, mending her bones, beating rivers in her blood. She is able to hear the voices, is beginning to want to sing the songs of those voices inside the earth. She tells her story in an unfaltering voice to a young, brown, lawyer, John Mercer Langston, who shakes with the fury of her story, who seems to draw his words from some unknown pit of empathy in the jurors. He reaches past the tombstones of guilt they have erected in their eyes and latches onto the truth they feel erupting from the small, battered frame sitting in the defendant's chair, and one day she limps out of the courtroom, emancipated. And soon, she is on her way away from Oberlin, away from Ohio, and then she is searching across the waters for the sound of stones calling her name.

MINNEHAHA

Edmonia Lewis, Marble, 1868

What part of me is mine that was
not mined from the mind of poets,
artists rewriting the past blow
by blow till it's pulverized past
the barely recognizable?
I was born when I was written,
then hammered out of a mountain.
I was shattered and then broken,
then sharpened to the human. I'm
carved in marble that never dies,
hardly crumbles; a stubborn queen
who'll die only with those people
who crave a ruling monarchy
of fictions—tales my sculptor plied
to strike against their pale armies
of indignities. History
is their favorite lie. I found
my face buried in its would-be
pages, then excavated by
a native who fled the country.
Such was her misery at home
in the land where my legend roams
the canonized American
poetry. I'm her stone arrow,
her refusal to bow. I wear
her chisel-sharp aim as my crown.

It is 1873 in Rome, and Wildfire has a new song in her hands right now, squirming in the alabaster clay she presses and kneads and molds. It is in the pulse of the marble that led her to leave Ohio, the sound of the Earth that drove her across the ocean. She was in search of a place to feel the earth sing its bonework of stone into her hands. And right now she can feel the muscle and tendon beneath the hardening clay. She holds it up to the daylight falling through her small studio. She has listened to the earth sing its story—she has listened with every inch of her body ready to break. She knows that mercy is hard and shining and distant, and she will pound and scrape and tear at the world until it sings its shape into her hands.

COLONEL ROBERT GOULD SHAW

Edmonia Lewis, Marble, 1865

The enemy buried me with my brothers
in blue. Our bloodlines mingled
in the mangled, makeshift ditch,
burrowed beneath sand and grit
to huddle in Earth's quarried
memory. We lay head to head,
bone to bone with eternity.
Then, her hands summoned me:
bade marble limn these eyes,
speak these lips. So, I face the world
again, wishing I could call my mon,
once more, to stand at attention . . .
Rigby, who'd drawl curses on Rebs
while drawing Colt revolvers;
Alison, who'd sworn not to die
till whipping his old master, his father,
before his freed mother's eyes;
Roper, his every inch mapped with lash-
marks that branded his route through hell . . .
and 1,100 more in the '54
with 1,100 blue-black stories to tell.
Her hands somehow searched out
each tale those men carved into my face,
scraping away marmoreal
myths that define which race

might rule. She cut dark witness
into this bust that carries forth
my image: proof that, in the end,
it's immortal stone that wins
when we're all dead and
finished.

The land of liberty had not room for a colored sculptor.

EDMONIA LEWIS: PROVENANCE

provenance. (n.) a record of ownership of a work of art,
used as a guide to authenticity or quality

Provenance is to Providence
as stone is to heaven,
as plinth is to bust,
as chisel is to muscle,
as beginning to end
that explodes into dust
for new beginnings.
I am the sound of one
mallet against history's
pale fist. I've birthed
apostles of eternal
prayer and protestation,
and I know how the dead
soldier's face ascends
from Earth's womb,
how a mother's prayer
weeps in the desert,
how the only questions
worth asking forever
appear impenetrable,
but break open beneath
a hammer-honed will. I will
my hands to my mother's
finger-weave, to all its angles

and the gods within each angle;
my eyes to river water
sculpting Time's ripple-smooth
face to boulder and shale;
my feet to my father's maroon,
broken bondage. I'm possessed
in the way of a warrior
feather, carved to sharpen
wind that weathers stone,
claiming the crown of all glory
that is myself, my own.

MT. SINAI BAPTIST CHURCH, WASHINGTON CO., GA, 2007: MACEDONIA CHURCH OF GOD IN CHRIST, SPRINGFIELD, MA, 2008: WARRIOR HILL BAPTIST CHURCH, PINE LEVEL, AL, 2011: NEW HOLY DELIVERANCE OUTREACH, AXTON, VA, 2013: FLOOD CHRISTIAN CHURCH, FERGUSON, MO, 2014:

WE'VE SUNG EACH FREE DAY
LIKE IT'S SALVATION

(CHORAL)

by hauling hand-me-down hymns 'cross every nation's

heart to prove black souls brightly human.

We fly on our God-given natural right

to shout ourselves into faith. We've braved through,

bellow-bound with an Almighty light

that tore down Jericho's walls. We seek a truth

that storms its way through whip-worn weather

like 'Zekiel's prayers sprouting before the wheel.

We've strapped our voice to our slaver's scripture

to loosen up chains from tangled cane fields.

We've sung smuggled faith from slave shack to palace,

boiling the air with hallelujah's balm—

each note bursting loose from bondage

to sing unto the world a new song.

CARSWELL-GROVE BAPTIST CHURCH, MILLEN, GA, 2014:

FIRST DELIVERANCE CHURCH, ST. ALBANS, WV, 2015

MOTHER EMMANUEL AME CHURCH, CHARLESTON, SC, 2015

April 1, 1927

Dear Sister Paula,

It's been quite a while since my last letter. I thank you for your patience. I am not deaf to your request for me to return. Believe me, I want to. I know the family needs me. But you must know that for me, return to Cairo is a chance I can't let myself take. I've seen too much of what Cairo means to me when I saw our cousin hanging from the lampposts, when I smelled the smoke they'd made of his flesh. I've chosen my Exodus, and looking back would burn me down to nothing but salt.

I continue here out on the road. However, I've seen all the rails have to offer a Negro, from the salvation and subservience found working as a Pullman Porter to the grit of a fireman's shovel tracing flame. I've seen the look on the engineer's face when he knows I know as much or more about running a train than he does, and I've read the headlines that tell how some Negro fireman got lynched because a white engineer was afraid for his job. As much as I've held my tongue for years, I know that the caprice of a white man scared for his job is as sharp as a hunting knife or slippery as a midnight "accident" that runs twelve tons of cargo wheel over an uppity spade. And, of course, I remember how Father gave everything he had to the hammer he swung on the rails, how he gave until there was nothing to get but a cut-rate casket.

And so, a few months ago when the train came to an unexpected stop, I looked at the tracks and all I could see was those rails running away from me. My life was being bent backwards one mile at a time without a single smile I could keep for myself. Not one shovelful of coal-black music was lifting my soul.

The night that I walked away from the 20th Century Limited, its engine had burned itself out. Although I'd advised that we overhaul the gaskets before we left Chicago, our engineer merely scowled and ordered us full speed ahead. We'd sweat ourselves down to the bone to keep her running. From axle pump and wheel bearings to side rods and crossheads we'd oiled her incessantly, stoked her furnace and coaxed every last mile out of her—until the main piston blew. We were stuck at a junction in a valley of dusking sun. There was no way to get her the next 30 miles into Akron until the relief engine arrived in another six hours.

I knew that my very presence was a rebuke to the engineer's haste. In search of solitude, at break time I walked out of the engine room to wash myself in the starlight. Way in the distance, in the direction of a tiny swarm of lamps, I could hear something that sounded like shouting. I scrambled down across the junction, across the head-high weeds, until a voice pushed through the darkness. I could hear it clearly, a barker shouting out to a small, growing audience. I could barely make out the sign above his head: *North Star Traveling Negro Troubadours.*

I watched them from the darkness of the weeds. The crowd flickered in the lamplight. Their faces shimmered in the shadows and let loose, from time to time, small broken guffaws and grins. They began clapping rhythm for a soft-shoed snake dancer. He made himself a top-hatted blur of limbs, roiling up a thunderstorm of heel-to-toe syncopation.

No one in the audience could see me buried in the shadow of the weeds. Not one human was there to observe my standing and staring in the junction. But there, perched high up on a platform that held the dancer's feet, was one sole witness to my wandering—a ragged upright. It was a refugee from ragtime days. We sat there, separated by darkness and distance, but together in mutual silence as the show went on. We sat watching each other, watching the worn-out comedy act, the jugglers, the clownish Sambo show. The piano was unattended, unplayed, and unadorned with sheets of music. It leaned to the right on its broken supports with a smirk, as if it knew the inside riddle behind each joke of the minstrels, how each line was carefully crafted to shadowbox myth.

Soon, the singer came up. Her "Steal Away" was ginned with cotton and cornmeal, and it was full of splinters always shifting into something smoother and new. But then she slowed down and sang Verdi like Mississippi was his birthright. After a pause, she let fly a blues that sliced itself out of misery's shackles and shined through to my gut. Even the limitless night wasn't enough to hold her song, and so the lamplights flickered harder in its wake.

It was in the middle of that voice soaring through the fields, through me, that I remembered that I still remembered who we are, P. I remembered those lessons Mama taught us, the rags she pulled out of the piano, how she wore herself out on each tune. Do you remember that? I do. I remember hearing all those tunes ring in and out of our house day after day, learning them by heart. Do you remember that, P? All the times she brought us up on the bench to hammer and tonk on that piano with her? How we got full on every note squeezed from that old husk of piano until we went to bed and raised up again in a morning that hummed? That's what I remember, P. That's what I remembered to remember.

And it was while standing right there that all those lessons rushed back at me. All the times I'd played that piano in the house after Mother died, cleansing myself from fury. All the times I'd played slowly in my head in my bunk after a thirty-hour Pullman run. Tracing keys when I had no keyboard in the French trenches with mortars constantly breaking Earth to bits. Fingering the fake piano board that was my cast in the hospital after I'd lost my face. That's what came back to me at the crossing between the train tracks and the troubadours.

I looked across the junction to the 20th Century, glowering in the distance. It was waiting for me like

10,000 miles of steel footsteps, churning its chamber full of scalding steam. I looked at it for a long time, P. Long enough to know I had fed so much of myself to its ever-hungry furnace that I had to turn away to save any scraps I had left. And so, I turned toward the tangle of upturned faces that surrounded the singer.

I walked slowly past them—past the low lamplight that cast the piano into shadow. The singer was deep into her song, a sweetcandied "St. Louis Blues." I climbed up from the darkness onto the piano's platform, and before anyone could stop me, I put my hands on the keys.

With my back to the audience, I bowed my head over the jaded ivories and softly joined in with the singer just as she approached the denouement of her song. I didn't look up to see her face, but I could just barely hear the surprise in her voice as I joined her on key. She broke stride a moment, but continued on through the song all the way till the end, leaving the crowd to search my back for answers as to how I got there and where I came from. But they all held off any questions for later, because the singer ended up asking me if I knew that new song, "Bye Bye Blackbird."

"I know enough of it," I said while hiding my face. And we went into it together, feeling each other out beneath the moths dancing in the kerosene shine.

It turned out that somehow I'd remembered enough of me to work that piano into something that moved like music. Something that sounded not exactly right, but right enough for that moment that played on for the rest of the night till just before dawn. It also turned out that their regular piano man had fallen off drunk a few stops back in Youngstown. Their manager, a small, cigar-smoking scrawl of a woman named Shoe, was in need. I thought maybe my appearance would be upsetting, but she doesn't mind my mask at all—she said that perhaps it let me know the true nature of the business. We struck a deal for me to stay on and hold that old piano down until a replacement was found. That was seven months ago, P.

I've struggled through most of the acts—but I've learned more and more from show to show. I'm the masked man of the caravan. The phantom of the minstrel show. This is a place where my mask affords me the appropriate degree of mystery. I'm a canvas upon which the audience paints their own story. Hero. Villain. Black. White. Sane. Mad. Wise man. Fool. I play each role every time I set myself down on that piano stool. I guess that's what I am, P. All of the above and more. That's what I imagine when I'm in front of those keys, anyway.

But don't worry, Sister. When the song-and-dance team crank up their act, when I can smell the cork burning just before the show, I still remember the dignity we were taught. Trust me, P. I haven't forgotten a thing. I still know who I am, even if my reflection is a lie. Even if the mask I wear to hide the scar the War to End All Wars made of my face is a lie. Even if no one back home would recognize this stitched-up pantomime of a face if I ever did wander back through Cairo's gates like some prodigal bruise.

Each day, I take a deep breath inside my mask to open myself up for the first part of the minstrel show. I play for the cakewalk exploding across the tiny stage. I play for the pickaninnies preening into the makeshift spotlight. I play the old ragtime smeared with dirty lyrics and the new blues songs smoldering like brothels underneath the singer's tongue. I play for our makeshift Tambo and Bones; I play for those in the audience that laugh for the joke before the joke's even over, mouthing the punch lines written in Tambo's blackface.

I play for the contortionist when he bends himself to fit the smallest of corners, and I play on to bend a waltz into tune with our singer's Georgia-bred ear. And through every note, I'm singing beneath my breath inside my mask, low enough for only me and my mask to hear. I sing while I play until the last of the last customers leaves. And then, because my fellow travelers have seen life far more twisted than what I have left for a face, because they seem to be able to see what was there before the mask was ever needed, I let the mask slip off beneath the starlight. After the shows are done, I bathe my naked face in their vision. I let them see what's left of me, and they know there's more to this battered scrap of flesh than meets the eye.

I chased a ghost once, P. The ghost of a man who made the music his castle and invited us inside and we turned his castle inside out even as he stood at the door deep in a bow that everyone took for servility. He died in the shadows of his own castle, and barely a soul stopped to note how he died. I hunted down whatever I could of his ghost and wrote it down because I thought that I could wear his face inside the stories I found for him. I was riding those rails, chasing his spirit, trying to make it my own, wanting to make the world the way it was.   But it won't be like that again, P. I know that now. I should've learned it from all those years with the sing and shuffle of the rails seeping into my bones. I should've learned it from the gandy-danced rhythm that Father hummed down to us, the way it lifted him up as a young man and then threw him down when it was done with him. But here I am, finally learning that lesson in this ragtag wandering across countryside; in the way the music slides off my fingers when I touch piano. I'm learning in the faces of our crowds from town to town to town that long to hear what note will come next.

I learn it over and over every time I sit at that barely playable piano at the edge of the stage. I learn everything about him and his journey that matters. And what matters is what I sing inside this mask when I play. It's whatever I sing when I'm rounding out the olio.

God bless, P. $10 enclosed here for your expenses. Spend well. Prayers.

JT

OLIO

APPENDIX
regarding facts and audience instruction
or
INTERLOCUTOR
interpreting during intermissions
or
BARKER'S BRIEF NOTES
Step Right Up!

THE DUNBAR-BOOKER DOUBLE SHOVEL

(PAGE 143)

Step Right Up:

Paul Dunbar and Booker T. bring their doubled shovels to work: to excavate the boundaries of pride and shuffle in syncopated verse: Dunbar's dialogue and Booker's intertwine and when combined it's a sculpture you'll find liberated from these bifurcated pages of history. "We Wear the Mask" lies lurking at the end of each column line—singing stichomythic backup twisting through time.

Create your own path through their side-by-side: start anywhere, and read them line-by-line, backward, forward, and diagonal-wise.

THUS:

This scarred, dark heritage. Listen. We dance it out daily. We
These painted-up faces, this minstreled-up hustle. Witness this:
promises unto ourselves not to die. That's when each of us eyes
escape into deceit's sanctuary. We've sheltered in each smile.

OR,

These painted-up faces, this minstreled-up hustle. Witness this:
This scarred, dark heritage. Listen. We dance it out daily. We
cast-off shadows in the soul that testify. We carry our debt:
everyday sacrifice like ceremonial celebration. We master the

Is it minstrelsy or is it pride—whose authority will decide the line between mask and the task of building Tuskegee? Not separated easily . . . Can you liberate their lines from the tyranny of two-dimensional reality? Cut them loose into three-dimensionality? Let them roll with a nation's lynchings scrolled up inside—and when you cut them loose along the dotted lines our speakers break out of their x/y axis grind to find the wonder of a rolling cylinder that reads back and forth and up and down, end of line into beginning into end again until there is no beginning . . .

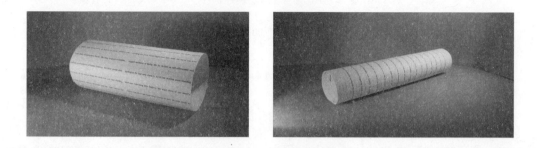

Still, there's more story to be told from the fixture of masks so flexible—find the caesura and make it fold so Dunbar and Booker are back to back against the stacked lynch mobs they hold inside—when you attach their ends once more, you'll find their tale told in torus form.

But there's more—one half twist before you join the torus will reveal the Möbius—a paradox poem on a two-dimensional surface but with one side that flips seamless from Dunbar to Booker and back again and again and again ad infinitum . . .

FOLDED   TORUS   MÖBIUS

  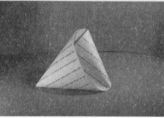

POSTSCRIPT:

Each singer also croons in their own circle independently.

As Dunbar will demonstrate:

We got our lies shinin' White folks on like spit-polished shoes.

And Booker will dissertate:

It's about bowing, and bestudded with built-in automatic smiles.

THE BERT WILLIAMS/GEORGE WALKER PARADOX

Bert and George step out the minstrel box with paradox. These verbal contortionists correlate and syncopate to emancipate themselves from two-dimensional postulates of blackface fate. "Jonah Man" Bert sings "Nobody" while George is the straight man dancing onstage. They call themselves "Two Real Coons" after seeing so many corked up white buffoons—they peddle the genuine article 'cause they know it'll sell (or so they snicker). They turn their backsides to Witmark's *Minstrel Guide* to hawk their hustle in this "syncopated ghazal," singing line by line, forward, backward, or on the diagonal.

And so . . .
Sing like me, Jonah in the charcoal hold of the whale—
just might be playing you for a fool. You see, this face
may be sung:
just might be playing you for a fool. You see, this face
Sing like me, Jonah in the charcoal hold of the whale—

Cut thru the dotted perforation to free the comedians from the medium of two dimensional tête-à-tête.

Take the last lines and loop them into the first. The jokesters will gently coax their heads and feet together so you can listen to them sing three dimensionally . . .

> *sure of the price—what our act's worth. Bet you nobody*
> *wise to the dark's risks. I'll shine the crowd. I'll have each face*
> *Sing like me, Jonah in the charcoal hold of the whale—*
> *Doing justice to my Juba jig. See how I dance?*

Follow their contrapuntal fellowship when they join side by side, hip to hip. Let 'em slide one seam against the other to hear their croonin' 'bout coonin' like . . .

> *be smilin' till the crowd starts to cry: this nobody*
> *just might be playing you for a fool. You see, this face*
>
> or
>
> *Can't help but see themselves beneath my blacked up face—*
> *might be sayin', "Look at dat handsome man!"*

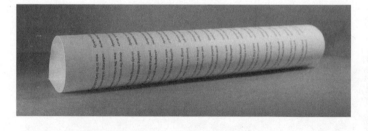
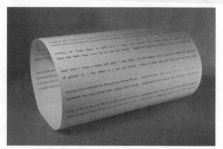

* * *

But when they fold along the caesura is when W/W rolls in real bravura. They'll hide the title that's above their heads down between their feet to mold the torus geometry. They'll even perform a Euclidian half-twist and bend into a Möbius. One's words flow into the other's and back again, and on and on like an ever-bending act, a joke that never (ever?) never ends.

TORUS   MÖBIUS

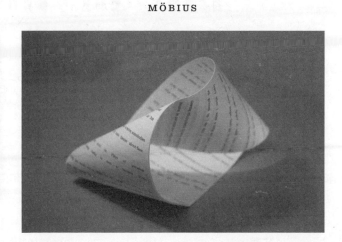

POSTSCRIPT:

Each comedian scrolls his own version with recursion.

Williams will self-collaborate:

Lil' fame don't hurt nobody speakin' low of my woe.

And Walker will self elaborate:

That's my mask, not my face, gettin' blistered with spotlight.

HENRY ''BOX'' BROWN FACING/ EVADING SLAVE CATCHER DREAM ON . . . DUET

(PAGE 76)

Our resident escape artist, Henry Brown, thinks outside the box to escape the town that held him hostage like a package bound by his opposing oppressor who curses and searches outside the crate Henry croons in. One faces the other—but then they face away when you liberate the page and attach them back-to-back so H can stare away and then again straight into the hate that seeks to read him up and down and can't wait to box him up. In the meantime this duo do their duet, unknowingly arguing through it diagonally, back and forth, up and down, and circlin' round with prayers of liberation and swears against emancipation: Witness their syncopation!

H: Coffined up in this here box. That's me. Henry:

SC: Tremblin' like a whip-torn waif! He'll arrive

H: Postage-paid freeman. I tell myself that I ain't

SC: Tremblin' like a whip-torn waif! He'll arrive

H: Coffined up in this here box. That's me. Henry:

SC: caught: sealed in slave chains again: He's a-

H: scared beyond death. Tell myself, *don't get baffled . . .*

And, dear friends, a blended amended quote from John Berryman's mind plays double shovel backup at the stichomythic end of every line. *'Cause now arrive a time* for old lit sins to get bent. As said before, let your scissors rend paper to illuminate this argument:

* * * * *

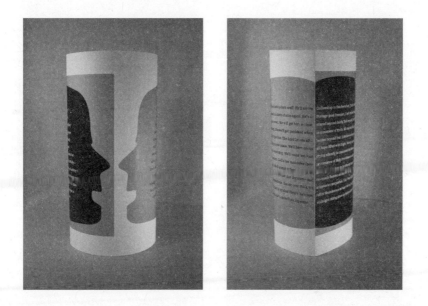

But we know how it ends in the end, audience—how Philly awaits Henry when he struggles out of his box of smuggle and strife to sing his hardest won act—his self-liberated life.

THE RESURRECTION OF HENRY BOX BROWN AT PHILADELPHIA.
Who escaped from Richmond Va. in a Box 3 feet long 2½ ft. deep and 2 ft. wide.

ON THE FISK JUBILEE CHOIR TESTIFYING THROUGH FIRE . . .

The names of our burned and bombed black churches enfold the spirituals sung by our Jubilee choir. Inside each flame burns hum, prayer, and holy book. Each hymn inhabits heat and smolder; each biblical spark is kindled with story. There is no complete record of all such attacks upon the black congregational body, no complete accounting of all the pulpits, pews and psalm books rendered into fire—these 148 stand in testimony to all the unnamed churches lost to arson and TNT, the slats and nails and sweat that doubled as schoolhouse and underground passageway, the pyres of pine and oak and cedar steeples that sheltered baptisms and home-goings, the silent crucifixions curled into ash. The AMEs and the Graces, the Tabernacles and all the many Firsts; the hand fans, tambourines, mourner's benches and collection plates; they rise in smoke like the songs that soaked through them and up to heaven's blued, eternal door.

ON THE CIRCULARITY OF SYNCOPATED SONNETS . . .

Syncopated sonnets sometimes sing in circles to allow recitation that'll roll interstitial, antigravitational, and diagonal, with voices splitting to each side but joining in the middle. Blind Tom does so in "One Body, Two Graves" and the Bethunes follow suit when "Introducing Blind Tom." Our dear McKoy sisters syncopate regularly with such sonnets. Here, the McKoys sing a snippet of their "Love Story" up/down, back/forth, and diagonal.

INTERSTITIAL . . .

Here—this is our story I want you to hear—
—one body crooning two notes. By God, we're
airborne, shook and shimmering through my head,
in a way very few could comprehend—
with every breath we've got. I'm filled completely,

OR

INTERSTITIAL/ANTIGRAVITATIONAL . . .

with every breath we've got. I'm filled completely,
in a way very few could comprehend—
airborne, shook and shimmering through my head,
—one body crooning two notes. By God, we're
Here—this is our story I want you to hear—

OR

DIAGONALLY DOWN AND THEN INTERSTITIALLY/

ANTIGRAVITATIONALLY UP . . .

Here—this is our story I want you to hear—
our own duet. Listen to how we're bound
—one body crooning two notes. By God, we're
ringing within me and my other half;
airborne, shook and shimmering through my head,
like sympathetic strings. Each sung sound
our own duet. Listen to how we're bound

Strike your own path through their lines. Circle round their stories to burrow through time.

THE TROTTER INTERVIEWS: JULIUS MONROE TROTTER, 1895–?

The Julius Trotter interviews were discovered by Jesse Byrd Jr. in 2012, lodged inside the forgotten compartment of a trunk that had been passed down to his mother, Frances Byrd. Mrs. Byrd had inherited the trunk from the estate of Miss Grace Shillady, her fraternal aunt and former secretary to W. E. B. Du Bois' *Crisis* magazine from 1922 to 1927.

Birth records indicate that Julius Trotter was born in Cairo, Illinois, to Gladys and Jasper Trotter in June of 1895. Jasper was a farmer and part-time Baptist minister, while Gladys was a former pianist with Callender's Georgia Minstrels who had settled down to become a piano instructor and laundress. Sadly, Gladys died of pneumonia when Julius was ten, leaving the family in dire financial straits. Further impoverished after the death of his father, Julius left Cairo after the infamous lynching of his cousin, Will "Froggy" James, in 1909. He fled to St. Louis, where he worked as an elevator operator and waiter. He later enrolled at Lincoln University. After earning his degree in 1915, he moved to Chicago where he joined the Pullman Palace Car Company as a porter.

In 1917, Julius joined the United States Army Expeditionary Force to fight with the Harlem Hellfighters 369th Infantry in World War I. While "defending an entrenched position from continuous concentrated enemy fire for eighteen hours" in the Battle of Belleau Wood (June 6–26, 1918) he suffered severe facial wounds. Julius was fitted with a prosthetic mask in France, was awarded an Inter-Allied Victor Medal, a Distinguished Service Cross, and received honorable discharge in 1919.

Unable to work again as a Pullman porter, Trotter found employment first as a fireman on the Great Northern and Susie Q (New York/Susquehanna/Western) lines, and later on the 20th Century Limited. This employment helped him travel about the states and conduct several interviews with former associates and friends of Scott Joplin.

Further details about Mr. Trotter are scant. The Trotter family has no account for him past 1927. A letter kept in the family Bible, Trotter's last known correspondence (doc. B: 4/1/27), indicates that he joined a traveling minstrel show, the North Star Traveling Negro Troubadours. Only one record of said troupe exists, a 1935 Works Progress Administration interview.

Family rumors about Mr. Trotter's fate vary. Some suggest that he eventually settled in New Orleans and played piano on and around Bourbon Street until the late 1930s. No records have been found to verify these accounts.

OLIO TIMELINE

African Methodist Episcopal Church founded.	**1816**	Henry "Box" Brown born in Luisa Co., VA.
Frederick Douglass escapes from slavery.	**1838**	George White, first director of Fisk Singers born.
Alexandre Dumas writes *The Three Musketeers*.	**1844**	Edmonia Lewis born in Greenbush, NY.
Dred Scott sues for his freedom; the 1857 decision will deny Blacks the right to sue.	**1846**	Ben Holmes, Fisk Jubilee Singers, born: Charleston, NC. Frederick Douglass starts *North Star* newspaper.
F. Douglass attends First Women's Rights Convention held in Seneca Falls, NY.	**1848**	Greene Evans, Fisk Jubilee Singers, born. H. "Box" Brown's wife, three children sold away.
Britain recognizes Liberia as independent state. Harriet Tubman escapes slavery, becomes a conductor on the Underground Railroad, and eventually frees more than 300 slaves.	**1849**	Tom "Blind Tom" Wiggins born: Harris Co., GA. Henry "Box" Brown escapes slavery in Virginia via crate shipped to Philadelphia. He publishes *Narrative of the Life of Henry Box Brown, Written by Himself*.
Fugitive Slave Law passed. Black Seminoles establish colony in Mexico.	**1850**	H. "Box" Brown moves to England, touring with his panorama, "Mirror of Slavery."
"Christiana Riot" in Christiana, PA: Black and White abolitionists successfully combat slave catchers trying to abduct four runaways.	**1851**	McKoy Twins born in Whiteville, NC. Ella Sheppard, of Fisk Jubilee Singers, born on Andrew Jackson's Hermitage plantation, TN.
Harriet Stowe's *Uncle Tom's Cabin* published. Frederick Douglass delivers his speech "What to the Slave Is the Fourth of July?"	**1852**	McKoy Twins leased to traveling freak show. Blind Tom's first musical composition, "The Rain Storm." Isaac Dickerson and Jennie Jackson born.
William Wells Brown publishes *Clotel; or, The President's Daughter*, to become the first African American novelist.	**1853**	Maggie Porter born in Lebanon, TN. McKoy Twins kidnapped to England, then rescued back to US with mother, Monemia.
Kansas-Nebraska Act repeals Missouri Compromise, opens new territories to slavery.	**1854**	Thomas Rutling, of Fisk Jubilee Singers, "best tenor in Tennessee," born in Wilson Co., TN.
John Brown's Battle of Black Jack in Kansas.	**1856**	Booker T. Washington born in Virginia.
Dred Scott decision declares Blacks non-citizens.	**1857**	Eliza Walker, Minnie Tate, of Fisk Jubilee Singers, born.

John Brown's raid on Harper's Ferry.	**1859**	Edmonia Lewis enrolls in Oberlin College.
Civil War declared.	**1861**	Blind Tom tours to raise funds for the
Black men form the 1st Louisiana		Confederacy under "management" of his
Native Guard of the Confederate Army.		master, "General" James Neil Bethune.
Anti-lynching activist Ida B. Wells born.	**1862**	Edmonia Lewis beaten; later exonerated after
Militia Act allows Blacks to serve in military.		a trial for poisoning classmates in Oberlin, OH.
Emancipation Proclamation signed.	**1863**	Robert Shaw killed with men of the MA 54th.
New York City Draft Riots.		Edmonia Lewis's first public exhibition.
Sherman's March to the Sea.	**1864**	John William "Blind" Boone born in Miami, MO.
Civil War ends. Reconstruction era begins.	**1865**	Ernest Hogan born in Bowling Green, KY.
Freedman's Bureau established.		Edmonia Lewis sails to Rome for sculpting.
Black men granted right to vote in Wash., DC.	**1867**	Scott Joplin born. Raised in Texarkana, AR.
W. E. B. Du Bois born.	**1868**	Sissleretta Jones born in Portsmouth, VA.
Civil Rights Act passed to guard Black suffrage.	**1871**	First Fisk Jubilee Singers tour.
First Nat'l Black Convention held in New Orleans.	**1872**	Paul Laurence Dunbar born.
150 Blacks murdered over voting rights	**1873**	Blind Boone runs away from MO School for the Blind.
in the Colfax Massacre of Louisiana.		George Walker of Fisk Jubilee Singers born.
Red River War clears free roaming Native	**1874**	Egbert Austin (Bert) Williams
Americans from Southwestern states.		born in Nassau, Bahamas.
Ulysses S. Grant signs the Civil Rights Act,	**1875**	Henry "Box" Brown returns to
which promises equal treatment for Blacks		America as mesmerist and showman.
in public accommodations, and preserves the		Ben Holmes, from the first Fisk
right to serve on juries; the legislation is		Jubilee Singers, dies in Nashville, TN.
struck down in 1883, and will not be more		Edmonia Lewis exhibits *The Death*
fully realized for nearly another century.		*of Cleopatra* in Centennial Exposition.
Seven Blacks killed in the Hamburg	**1876**	President Grant commissions
Massacre in Hamburg, SC.		Edmonia Lewis for a portrait.
Reconstruction ends, and the last Union	**1877**	Blind Boone kidnapped by an "agent"
troops are withdrawn from the South.		and recovered by his stepfather.
Nearly all the civil rights gained		Blind Tom meets McKoy Twins.
during Reconstruction are eliminated.		Last known appearance of H. "Box" Brown.
Jack Johnson, first African American	**1878**	Greene Evans, of the first Fisk Jubilee
Heavyweight Boxing Champion, born.		Singers, elected to Memphis City Council.

Mass exodus from Texas of 12,000 "Exoduster"	**1879**	Marshfield, MO., tornado kills 100 people;
freed Blacks to Kansas and Missouri.		Blind Boone writes "Marshfield Tornado."
Booker T. Washington appointed head of Tuskegee	**1881**	James Reese Europe born in Mobile, AL.
Institute in Tuskegee, AL.		Scott Joplin moves to Sedalia, MO.
51 Black Americans reported lynched.	**1884**	Jennie Jackson forms DeHart Jubilee Club.
74 Black Americans reported lynched.	**1885**	Greene Evans, of the first Fisk Jubilee Singers
Death of author and activist Martin Delaney.		elected to Tennessee General Assembly.
94 Black Americans lynched.	**1889**	Blind Tom meets Blind Boone for piano duet.
169 Blacks reported lynched.	**1892**	Sissieretta Jones performs at Carnegie Hall.
118 Blacks reported lynched.	**1893**	Bert Williams and George Walker
Daniel Hale Williams performs first		form comedy duo Two Real Coons.
successful open-heart surgery in Chicago.		Paul Dunbar's first book, *Oak and Ivy*.
Booker T. Washington's Atlanta Exposition Speech.	**1895**	George White, first director of Fisk choir, dies.
113 Blacks reported lynched.		Julius Monroe Trotter born in Cairo, IL.
Plessy v. Ferguson upholds "separate but	**1896**	Sissieretta Jones forms Black Patti Troubadours.
equal" doctrine, legalizes racial segregation.		Ernest Hogan writes "All Coons Look Alike to Me."
National Assoc. of Colored Women's Clubs founded.		Joplin's "Crush Collision March" published.
78 Blacks reported lynched.		Dunbar publishes *Lyrics of Lowly Life*.
127 Blacks reported lynched.	**1897**	Scott Joplin publishes "Maple Leaf Rag."
85 Blacks reported lynched.	**1899**	Joplin marries first wife, Belle Hayden.
12 Blacks killed in New Orleans Race Riot.	**1900**	Isaac Dickerson, of Fisk Jubilee Singers, dies.
106 Blacks reported lynched.		Joplin's infant daughter dies. Joplin divorces.
105 Blacks reported lynched.	**1901**	Bert Williams and George Walker
Booker T. Washington publishes *Up From*		record for Victor Records and become
Slavery and dines with Pres. Teddy Roosevelt.		world's first Black recording artists.
84 Blacks reported lynched.	**1903**	Bert Williams and George Walker produce
W. E. B. Du Bois publishes *Souls of Black Folk*.		Broadway musical-comedy hit *In Dahomey*.
76 Blacks reported lynched.	**1904**	Scott Joplin's second wife, Freddie, dies.
W. E. B. Du Bois organizes Niagara Movement.	**1905**	Scott Joplin publishes "Bethena," his first
57 Blacks reported lynched.		composition after the death of Freddie.
62 Blacks reported lynched.	**1906**	Paul Laurence Dunbar dies in Dayton, OH.
Alain Locke is first Black Rhodes Scholar.	**1907**	Scott Joplin moves to New York.
Edwin Harleston founds *Pittsburgh Courier*.		Edmonia Lewis dies near London, England.

89 Blacks reported lynched.	**1908**	Blind Tom dies in Hoboken, NJ, as "ward"
Springfield Race Riot kills two Blacks.		of Eliza Bethune, widow of Tom Bethune.
W. E. B. Du Bois founds Natl. Assoc. for	**1909**	Lynching of William James in Cairo, IL.
Advancement of Colored People.		Julius Monroe Trotter leaves Cairo for Fisk.
67 Blacks reported lynched.	**1910**	Jennie Jackson, of first Fisk
First issue of *The Crisis* magazine		Jubilee Singers, dies in Cincinnati.
published with Du Bois as editor.		James Reese Europe founds Clef Club in NYC.
60 Blacks reported lynched.	**1911**	George Walker dies. Joplin self-publishes.
W. C. Handy publishes "Memphis Blues."	**1912**	McKoy Twins die together, in North Carolina.
Marcus Garvey establishes the	**1914**	Joplin's *Treemonisha* critically praised
Universal Negro Improvement Association.		as "entirely new form of operatic art."
World War I begins in Europe.		Death of Greene Evans (bass),
51 Blacks reported lynched.		and Ella Sheppard (soprano).
The Birth of a Nation debuts, screens in the White	**1915**	Thomas Rutling, Fisk Jubilee Singers, dies.
House, and helps inspire resurgence of KKK.		Joplin mounts *Treemonisha* with limited
Booker T. Washington dies in Tuskegee, AL.		budget in small New Jersey theater.
US enters World War I.	**1917**	Scott Joplin dies in New York City,
James Reese Europe forms 369th		April 1, at Manhattan State Hospital.
Infantry Harlem Hellfighters Jazz Band.		Julius Trotter joins 369th Infantry.
World War I Armistice: troops return home.	**1918**	Julius Trotter injured in Battle of Belleau Wood.
Red Summer: 26 race riots across America.	**1919**	Julius Trotter recuperates in hospital, France.
James Reese Europe records "On Patrol in No Man's Land."		James Reese Europe killed by his drummer.
Anti-lynching bill killed in Senate. 51 lynched.	**1922**	Bert Williams dies in New York.
Marcus Garvey deported from US.	**1927**	"Blind" Boone dies in Warrensburg, MO.
The Jazz Singer, first movie with sound,		Julius Trotter mails interviews to
starring Al Jolson as a minstrel, opens.		*The Crisis* and mails a letter to his sister.
King Kong debuts.	**1933**	Sissieretta Jones dies in Providence, RI.
Congress of Racial Equality founded in Chicago.	**1942**	Maggie Porter, first Fisk Jubilee Singers, dies.
First National Black Political Convention	**1972**	*Treemonisha* launched as full-scale
held in Gary, IN. John Berryman dies.		production by Houston Grand Opera.
Reelection of First Black President, Barack Obama.	**2012**	Discovery of Julius Monroe Trotter interviews.

BIBLIOGRAPHY

Abbott, Lynn and Doug Seroff. *Out of Sight: The Rise of African American Popular Music, 1889–1895*. Jackson: University Press of Mississippi, 2002.

——. *Ragged but Right: Black Traveling Shows, "Coon Songs," and the Dark Pathway to Blues and Jazz*. Jackson: University Press of Mississippi, 2007.

Badger, Reid. *A Life in Ragtime: A Biography of James Reese Europe*. New York: Oxford University Press, 1995.

Berlin, Edward A. *King of Ragtime: Scott Joplin and His Era*. New York: Oxford University Press, 1994.

——. *Ragtime: A Musical and Cultural History*. Berkeley: University of California Press, 1980. Reprint, Authors Guild Backinprint.com, 2002.

Berryman, John. *The Dream Songs*. New York: Farrar, Straus and Giroux, 1969.

Brooks, Daphne A. *Bodies in Dissent: Spectacular Performances of Race and Freedom, 1850–1919*. Durham: Duke University Press, 2006.

Brown, Henry. *Narrative of the Life of Henry Box Brown, Written by Himself*. Manchester, England: Lee and Glynn, 1851.

Buick, Kirsten Pai. *Child of the Fire: Mary Edmonia Lewis and the Problem of Art History's Black and Indian Subject*. Durham: Duke University Press, 2010.

Davenport, Christian. *Burning God's House*. Accessed April 1, 2015. http://strangefruitinc.com/Strange_Fruit/Church_Burnings,_1989–1996.html.

Dumont, Frank. *The Witmark Amateur Minstrel Guide and Burnt Cork Encyclopedia*. New York: M. Witmark & Sons, 1899. Revised 1905.

Forbes, Camille F. *Introducing Bert Williams: Burnt Cork, Broadway, and the Story of America's First Black Star*. New York: Basic Civitas, 2008.

Frost, Linda. *Conjoined Twins in Black and White: The Lives of Millie-Christine McKoy & Daisy and Violet Hilton*. Madison: University of Wisconsin Press, 2009.

Harrah, Madge. *Blind Boone: Piano Prodigy*. Minneapolis: Carolrhoda Books, 2004.

Henderson, Harry and Albert Henderson. *The Indomitable Spirit of Edmonia Lewis: A Narrative Biography*. Milford, CT: Esquiline Hill Press, 2012.

Jacques, Geoffrey. *A Change in the Weather: Modernist Imagination, African American Imaginary*. Amherst: University of Massachusetts Press, 2009.

Jasen, David A. and Gene Jones. *Spreadin' Rhythm Around: Black Popular Songwriters, 1880–1930*. New York: Routledge, 2005.

Library of Congress. "Timeline of African American History, 1852–1925." Accessed April 1, 2015. http://memory.loc.gov/ammem/aap/aaphome.html.

Lott, Eric. *Love & Theft: Blackface Minstrelsy and the American Working Class*. New York: Oxford University Press, 1995.

Martell, Joanne. *Millie-Christine: Fearfully and Wonderfully Made*. Winston-Salem: John F. Blair, 2000.

McKoy, Millie-Christine *The History of the Carolina Twins. Told in "Their Own Peculiar Way" by "One of Them."* Buffalo: Buffalo Courier Printing House, year unknown. Accessed April 1, 2015. http://docsouth.unc.edu/neh/millie-christine/millie-christine.html.

O'Connell, Deirdre. *The Ballad of Blind Tom, Slave Pianist: America's Last Musical Genius*. New York: Overlook Press, 2009.

Riis, Thomas L. *Just Before Jazz: Black Musical Theater in New York, 1890–1915*. Washington, DC: Smithsonian Institution Press, 1989.

Ruggles, Jeffrey. *The Unboxing of Henry Brown*. Richmond: Library of Virginia, 2003.

Southern, Eileen. *The Music of Black Americans: A History*. 3rd ed. New York: W. W. Norton, 1997.

Story, Rosalyn M. *And So I Sing: African-American Divas of Opera and Concert.* New York: Warner Books, 1990.

Strain, Christopher B. *Burning Faith: Church Arson in the American South*. Gainesville: University Press of Florida, 2008.

Student Nonviolent Coordinating Committee, "Mississippi Bombings Since June 10, 1964. October 5, 1964." Ellin (Joseph and Nancy) Freedom Summer Collection, University of Southern Mississippi Libraries. Accessed April 1, 2015. http://digilib.usm.edu/cdm/compoundobject/collection/manu/id/871/rec/42

Tolnay, Stewart E. and E. M. Beck. *A Festival of Violence: An Analysis of Southern Lynchings, 1882–1930*. Urbana and Chicago: University of Illinois Press, 1995.

Trotter, James M. *Music and Some Highly Musical People* (1878). New York: Johnson Reprint Corporation, 1968.

Waldo, Terry. *This Is Ragtime*. 1st ed., New York: Da Capo Press, 1976; "enhanced republication," New York: Jazz at Lincoln Center Library Editions, 2009.

Ward, Andrew. *Dark Midnight When I Rise: The Story of the Jubilee Singers Who Introduced the World to the Music of Black America*. New York: Farrar, Straus and Giroux, 2000.

Wondrich, David. *Stomp and Swerve: American Music Gets Hot, 1843–1924*. Chicago: A Cappella Books, 2003.

Afro-American. 1926. City Edition. May 1.

——. 1930. "Church Burned 3 Times by Underworld Now Worth $350,000." November 8.

——. 1962. "3 in Church Arson Draw 7-Year Term." October 6.

Atlanta Daily World. 1935. "Church Burned in Egg Harbor." June 6.

——. 1962. "Four Confess Burning Church in Downing, GA." September 18.

Butler, Sheryl M. "Black Church Burned." *Chicago Daily Defender*. November 7, 1970.

Carey, Daniel. "Capture Of Sam Hose Seems To Be Matter Of Only A Few Hours." *Atlanta Constitution*. April 15, 1899.

Chicago Daily Defender. 1962. "Donate $11,000 to Fund for 3 Burned Churches." September 17.

——. 1963. "Believes Racist Burned Church." December 24.

——. 1965. "7 Free in Dixie Church Arson." November 6.

——. 1967. "Whites Accused of Mississippi Church Arson." January 24.

Christian Observer. 1900. "Our Colored Work." February 21.

City Edition. 1940. "Burner of Negro Church Found Guilty: Jury Convicts White Farmer in North Carolina." March 23.

Cleveland Call and Post. 1957. "Church Burned." May 25.

Coleman, Robert. "As Hate-Inspired Terror Stalks through South Carolina . . ." *New Journal and Guide*. October 22, 1955.

Cutts, Beau. "Fires Level 4 Black Churches." *Atlanta Constitution*. December 19, 1977.

Daily Defender. 1957. "Query Student in Church Arson." August 7.

Marian, F. D. "Chicago Church Burned In Political Campaign." *Pittsburgh Courier*. April 16, 1927.

Philadelphia Tribune. 1915. "Men Whipped Church Burned." February 20.

Pittsburgh Courier. 1947. "Two Schools, Church Burned." December 6.

Washington, Betty. "Cops See Racial Angle in Church Arson Bombing." *Chicago Daily Defender*. April 6, 1967.

Williams, Lamar. "Fire Destroys Harrisburg's 2nd Oldest Black Church." *Philadelphia Tribune*. November 28, 1995.

ACKNOWLEDGMENTS

Work in *Olio* has been printed in the following journals:

ACADEMY OF AMERICAN POETS POEM-A-DAY

"Hagar in the Wilderness"

THE AMERICAN POETRY REVIEW

"Bert Williams/George Walker Paradox"

BOMB

"Blind Boone's Pianola Blues"

CALLALOO

"Coon Songs Must Go!/ Coon Songs Go On (1)"

"Coon Songs Must Go!/ Coon Songs Go On (2)"

"Coon Songs Must Go!/ Coon Songs Go On (3)"

Fisk Jubilee Song of Sonnets: "Jubilee Proclamation (choral)," "Jubilee Blues (choral),"

"Isaac Dickerson,""Eliza Walker," "Ben Holmes," "Minnie Tate," "George White,"

"Maggie Porter," "Greene Evans," "Ella Sheppard," "Thomas Rutling," "Jennie Jackson,"

"Jubilee Indigo (choral)," "Jubilee Mission (choral)," "We've sung each day free like it's

salvation (choral)" (published as "We show from day to day his salvation (choral)")

"Provenance"

"Minnehaha"

"Colonel Robert Gould Shaw"

"My Name is Sissieretta Jones"

"O patria mia"

CONNOTATION PRESS: AN ONLINE ARTIFACT

(Connotationpress.com)

"Blind Tom Plays for Confederate Troops, 1863"

"What Marked Tom?"

"Blind Tom Plays for a Packed House, 1873"

"What the Wind, Rain, and Thunder Said to Tom"

"Charity on Blind Tom"

"General Bethune on Blind Tom"

"Blind Tom plays on . . ."

CURA: A LITERARY MAGAZINE OF ART AND ACTION

"Interview: Sam Patterson on Scott Joplin"

"Interview: Della Marie Jenkins on Scott Joplin"

INDIANA REVIEW

"Blind Tom: One Body, Two Graves; Brooklyn/Georgia"

"Duet: Blind Boone Meets Blind Tom, 1889"

"Mark Twain v. Blind Tom"

"General Bethune v. W. C. Handy"

"Millie McKoy & Christine McKoy Recall Meeting Blind Tom, 1877"

JUBILAT

"Mirror of Slavery/Mirror Chicanery"

"Pre/face: Berryman/Brown"

"Freedsong: Dream Gone"

"Freedsong: Dream Dawn"

"Freedsong: So Long! (Duet)"

"Freedsong: Dream Long"

"Freedsong: Of 1850"

"Freedsong: Dream Wronged"

"Freedsong: Dream of My Son"

"Freedsong: Dream Strong"

"Freedsong: Of 1876"

"Freedsong: Dream Song"

KINFOLKS: A JOURNAL OF BLACK EXPRESSION

"Blind Boone's Rage"

MATHEMATICAL PATTERN POETRY

"Bert Williams/George Walker Paradox"

NASHVILLE REVIEW

"Blind Tom Plays for Confederate Troops, 1863"

"What Marked Tom?"

"Blind Tom Plays for a Packed House, 1873"

"What the Wind, Rain, and Thunder Said to Tom"

"Charity on Blind Tom"

"General Bethune on Blind Tom"

"Blind Tom plays on . . ."

POETRYNET *POET OF THE MONTH, OCTOBER 2012*

"Bert Williams/George Walker Paradox"

"Mark Twain v. Blind Tom"

TAOS JOURNAL OF INTERNATIONAL POETRY AND ART

"Blind Boone's Blessings"

"Blind Boone's Escape"

"Blind Boone's Rage"

"My Name Is Sissieretta Jones"

"O patria mia"

"Sissieretta Jones: forte/grazioso"

This book was a long series of stagger and stumble and getting up off the ground again. Thanks to my mom and dad, Della Mae McGraw and Jesse F. Goodwin, for giving me the start to be able to finish this book.

Also, thanks to so many who listened to my worries and worked through my slow, slow hand during the years spent completing this book. All of Cave Canem's wild, mischievous, brilliant collective soul and brain. The inspiration of Sterling Plumpp and Herbert Woodward Martin. All the folks that read parts of this book and helped by hollering their hurrahs and hesitations . . . Patrick Rosal, Tonya Foster, Rigoberto Gonzalez, Courtney Bryan, Reginald R. Robinson, Tayari Jones, Nina Mercer, Randall Horton, MK Lewis, Ekere Tallie, Malika Booker, Van Jordan, Cate Marvin, Pat Smith, Willie Perdomo, Jeffrey Renard-Allen, Leslie Youngblood, Quincy and Margaret Troupe, Vievee Francis, Duriel Harris, TS Ellis, Bridgett Davis, Quraysh Lansana, Niki Herd, Marilyn Nelson, Kelly Shepard, Hermine Pinson, Reginald Harris, Evie Shockley, David Mills, Lee Jenkins, Heidi Broadhead, Matthew Zapruder, Joshua Beckman, and David Caligiuri.

Thanks also go to the intrepid folk at Wave Books, who believed in this manuscript and brought it home.

This book is dedicated to all the musicians in the Black tradition who lent their breath and muscle to the unique joy and discipline of their art forms—who never had their sounds recorded for posterity.